Wagner at Home

JUDITH GAUTIER

TRANSLATED BY
EFFIE DUNREITH MASSIE

CAMBRIDGE
UNIVERSITY PRESS

CAMBRIDGE
UNIVERSITY PRESS

University Printing House, Cambridge, CB2 8BS, United Kingdom

Cambridge University Press is part of the University of Cambridge.

It furthers the University's mission by disseminating knowledge in the pursuit of
education, learning and research at the highest international levels of excellence.

www.cambridge.org
Information on this title: www.cambridge.org/9781108078214

This edition first published 1910
This digitally printed version 2015

ISBN 978-1-108-07821-4 Paperback

CAMBRIDGE LIBRARY COLLECTION

Books of enduring scholarly value

Music

The systematic academic study of music gave rise to works of description, analysis and criticism, by composers and performers, philosophers and anthropologists, historians and teachers, and by a new kind of scholar - the musicologist. This series makes available a range of significant works encompassing all aspects of the developing discipline.

Wagner at Home

Daughter of the poet Théophile Gautier, Judith Gautier (1845–1917) grew up among Europe's literary avant-garde, quickly establishing her own career as a writer. An unapologetic admirer of Richard Wagner from an early age, she described her moment of revelation on playing through the overture to *The Flying Dutchman* as 'vertigo of the spirit'. Her enthusiasm led to several works on the composer, including a translation of his poem for *Parsifal*, during the composition of which an intense intimacy developed between them (gently, but firmly, defused by Cosima). Reissued here is the 1910 English translation by Effie Dunreith Massie of Gautier's highly charged account of her first two visits to Wagner and Cosima in Switzerland in 1869 and 1870. Gautier describes the idyllic atmosphere and offers the reader an effusive pen-portrait of Wagner's complex personality. The work also features facsimile pages of Wagner's letters to Gautier, showing part of the score for *Parsifal*.

Cambridge University Press has long been a pioneer in the reissuing of out-of-print titles from its own backlist, producing digital reprints of books that are still sought after by scholars and students but could not be reprinted economically using traditional technology. The Cambridge Library Collection extends this activity to a wider range of books which are still of importance to researchers and professionals, either for the source material they contain, or as landmarks in the history of their academic discipline.

Drawing from the world-renowned collections in the Cambridge University Library and other partner libraries, and guided by the advice of experts in each subject area, Cambridge University Press is using state-of-the-art scanning machines in its own Printing House to capture the content of each book selected for inclusion. The files are processed to give a consistently clear, crisp image, and the books finished to the high quality standard for which the Press is recognised around the world. The latest print-on-demand technology ensures that the books will remain available indefinitely, and that orders for single or multiple copies can quickly be supplied.

The Cambridge Library Collection brings back to life books of enduring scholarly value (including out-of-copyright works originally issued by other publishers) across a wide range of disciplines in the humanities and social sciences and in science and technology.

WAGNER AT HOME

Richard Wagner.

WAGNER AT
HOME

FULLY TRANSLATED BY

EFFIE DUNREITH MASSIE

FROM THE FRENCH OF

JUDITH GAUTIER

WITH NINE ILLUSTRATIONS

MILLS & BOON, LIMITED
49 RUPERT STREET
LONDON W.

Published 1910

TURNBULL AND SPEARS, PRINTERS, EDINBURGH

LIST OF ILLUSTRATIONS

WAGNER AT HOME

PART FIRST

I

THE train moved slowly, as becomes a well-conducted Swiss train that winds through beautiful country, and has no intention of blurring the views by undue haste. At each station there was a long stop, a slow renewal of leisurely motion.

To our little company of impatient French people within the compartment this slow progress was very trying. A feverish excitement possessed us ; we could not sit still ; from time to time we thrust our heads between the curtains to gaze in advance of the train. Villiers de l'Isle-Adam was one of us and most enthusiastic of all, his emotion continually bubbling over into spasmodic laughter and disjointed phrases.

On an ordinary excursion this slowness of the train would not have troubled us—but to-day—to-day we were going to Lucerne to see for the first time—Richard Wagner !

The swiftest " Express " would have seemed slow to us, yet we half dreaded the moment of arrival—when we should see the Master, hear him, speak to him !

What this wonderful genius meant to us it would have been difficult to make clear to those who were not of us, at that time when only a little group of disciples stood by the Master upholding him against the jeers of the masses who failed to comprehend him. Even to-day, when the triumph of the cause we supported has surpassed our hopes, it is not easy to explain our exaltation. We had the fanaticism of priests and martyrs—even to the slaying of our adversaries! It would, in fact, have been impossible to convince us that we should not be entirely justified in annihilating all those scoffers—blind to the new radiance which was so clear to us.

Each Sunday, when Pasdeloup played selections from Wagner, Homeric defiances were hurled between the opposing camps in the body of the concert hall and the interference of the town-guard was often required to prevent actual hand-to-hand conflict.

We had never dreamed that one day we should

look upon the face of the Master. He was for us as inaccessible as Jupiter on the heights of Olympus or Jehovah behind the flaming triangle, yet now we were going to him !

" It is to you, my dear Judith, that we owe this incredible good fortune," exclaimed Villiers, throwing himself upon the seat beside me and pressing my hand between both his own.

In truth it was due to me, and my pride in the fact would not allow me to make light of it.

For, carried away by my enthusiasm and relying upon my instinct alone, I had had the audacity a few months before to publish a series of articles upon Richard Wagner. I had done this with a truly French impulsiveness, as I had then heard only a few fragments, indifferently rendered by orchestra, of all his stupendous work. I had even dared to attack an article upon Glück and Wagner, published by Earnest Reyer, a friend who had known me from my babyhood, and who was amazed by such unexpected aggression—truly youth stops at nothing —he had, however, replied very courteously, and this musical passage of arms had created some little sensation.

After much hesitation I had sent the articles to Wagner—then at Lucerne—and with them a letter in which I begged him to forgive and to correct whatever errors there might be. Then, with what trepidation I looked and longed for a reply! Would he write?—I could hardly hope for that. Yet I suffered a pang of disappointment each morning when the postman came and went, leaving no longed-for letter. One day, at last, I saw an envelope bearing a Lucerne stamp and an unfamiliar handwriting which I nevertheless knew at once. With what emotions, and in what fear and trembling I opened it. Could it be possible?—Four whole pages of fine, close writing, clear and elegant, and below the last line the magic signature! . . . Here is the letter :—

" MADAME,—You cannot imagine the kindly and touching impression that your letter and your beautiful articles have made upon me. Permit me to thank you and to count you among the very few true friends whose far-seeing sympathy makes my only glory. I have found nothing to correct or to alter in your articles ; only I see that you do not yet know the *Meistersinger* very intimately. The introduction to the third act has really appealed to our public. My barber told me the other day that this part pleased him most of all, which led me to reflect that the instincts of the people can neither be measured nor comprehended.

" As the curtain rises upon this third act, Hans Sachs, the cobbler, is seen in his workshop, early in the morning, seated in his arm-chair, entirely absorbed by his reading of the 'Chronicle' of the world. He speaks to his young apprentice, without interrupting the profound concentration of his mind upon his book.

" After the departure of the boy, he remains with head bowed over his enormous volume, and his meditation, silent up to this point, finally finds expression in these words spoken aloud, '*Wahn, Wahn! überall Wahn!*' I do not know how to translate this, because '*Vanity, Vanity! All is vanity!*' does not give the exact meaning of *Wahn*, which is much more general, and expresses the object of the folly as well as the folly itself.

" God only knows how my public divined,

from the instrumental introduction to the third act, the situation that followed and the spiritual state of my Hans Sachs.

" It is true that in the second act, during the third verse of the shoemaker's song, the first motif of the stringed instruments had been introduced, suggesting there the hidden bitterness of the all-enduring man who reveals to the world only a cheerful and energetic front.

" Eva had comprehended this secret grief, and, moved to the depth of her soul, she had longed to fly where she could no longer hear that song with its pretence of joy.

" Here [1] this motif is played alone and developed fully, to die away at last in the sadness of renunciation, but, at the same time, the horns take up, softly, as if heard from a distance, the solemn chant with which Hans Sachs saluted Luther and the Reformation, and which brought to the poet a supreme popularity.   After the first strophe the stringed instruments retake softly, and in a very slow movement, the themes of the true song of the shoemaker, as if the man raised his head from the work of his trade to look upward

---

[1] In the introduction to the third act.

and lose himself in sweet and tender reveries. Then the horns, with their most exalted tone, break in triumphantly with that hymn of the Master with which Hans Sachs, on his appearance at the Fête in the third act, is saluted by all the people of Nuremberg in one unanimous thunder of applause.

" Again, the first motif of the stringed instruments enters, expressing with vigour the natural emotion of a soul profoundly moved. Gradually it grows calmer and more serene, and finally arrives at the supreme peace of a sweet and beautiful resignation.

" It is the real meaning of this short instrumental part that so impressed the worthy Pasdeloup that he essayed to perform it at your concerts as an illustration of this unusual music.

" Pardon me, Madame, for venturing to complete, with the aid of my imperfect French, your knowledge of my music—a knowledge otherwise so thorough and profound as truly to have surprised and touched me.

" I shall probably go to Paris before long, perhaps even this winter, and I delight in the anticipation of the real pleasure of taking your

hand and telling you in person what good you
have done to your very grateful and sincere,

"RICHARD WAGNER."

Wagner did not come to Paris that winter,
so I looked for him in vain. But my longing
to see him had become irresistible since the Master
had written that he would like to know me.

There was only one thing to do—to go to
Lucerne. But how should I be received?
Strange stories were told about Wagner. One
authority reported that he had a seraglio of
women of all countries and of all colours, clothed
magnificently, but that no one ever crossed his
threshold.

Someone else described him as an unsociable
man, gloomy and disagreeable, living alone in
strict seclusion, his only companion a great black
dog. . . .

The idea of this stern solitude was not incon-
gruous, and rather pleased me ; but I was greatly
troubled lest the Master might feel forced to permit
my intrusion only through some sentiment of
gratitude or courtesy.

Therefore I wrote a rather complicated letter,

saying that I should pass through Lucerne with some friends, on my way to an exhibition of paintings at Munich. It would be only a flying visit, I wrote, and I begged him to tell me if he would be there at that time, and if I might go to pay my respects to him.

He would understand from this that I should not disturb him by staying too long.

The following letter completely reassured me :—

" MADAME,—I am now in Lucerne, and I need not tell you how glad I shall be to see you. But can I not persuade you to prolong your stay in Lucerne for a little, in order that the pleasure you grant me may not be too soon over ?

" I suppose that you are going to Munich for the exhibition of paintings ; yet, as I venture to believe that you would be glad to hear some one of my works, I must tell you that the representations of *Tannhäuser*, *Lohengrin*, *Tristan*, and the *Meistersinger* took place in the month of June ; the theatre is closed at present, and the *Rheingold* will not be given before the 25th August, if, indeed, it is given at all.

" But I hope that neither the postponement of the exhibition nor the closing of the theatre will delay your visit to Lucerne; on the contrary, I shall hope that your stay here may be prolonged.

" Please send me a line, telling me the day of your arrival, and accept again the assurance of my sincere regard.

" RICHARD WAGNER."

By an exchange of telegrams I was assured that the Master would also welcome my companions, like myself his ardent disciples—and off we started.

The last night we slept at Basle, where we had an adventure which made a vivid impression upon us all. We arrived at night, and after dining, we attempted to see what we could of the city, in spite of the darkness. We found ourselves in a maze of narrow streets, dimly lighted at long intervals. Rather bewildered, we went on across thoroughfares and squares where large fountains could be seen, only to find ourselves again in narrow lanes.

At last we emerged into a wide, open place, which the sky helped to make a little lighter; a deep and continuous roaring pervaded it, which quite appalled us, and made us advance with great precaution. This tremendous volume of sound was produced by the Rhine. It is very wide at this point and rushes through Basle with the violence of a torrent.

Stopping in the middle of the bridge, we leaned over the parapet, and watched the ink-black river hurling itself on into the night, bearing with it the shattered reflections of the stars, and seeming to long to carry away the bridge also, and even the city.

A large moon, red as glowing embers, rose above the gables and irregular outlines of the houses along the river-bank. It cast across the river a crimson trail, which was wildly tossed and scattered by the waves.

We lingered there, spell-bound by this sight, when, suddenly, we heard a song, that seemed to rise clear and strong out of the tumult of waters. Could we be dreaming? It was well known to us. The sailors' song from *The Flying Dutchman*. What! Did that ill-omened ship come to roam by night upon this impassable stream? Bending lower, we peered into the

black water, but we could see nothing ; yet now
the voices were very near—it seemed as if the
invisible ship were passing under the arch of the
bridge itself.

We were greatly agitated, but when the voices
were silent, we went away without wishing to
fathom the mystery, shunning the possible discovery of some cheerful tavern concealed in a
recess of the high bank, where lusty Swiss peasants
found shelter, and grouped about their mugs
of foaming beer, sang with their clear, sonorous
voices the song that had so mystified us.

Now, while the train crept along, we recalled
this episode of our pilgrimage, and it seemed to
us a happy omen.

For the first time we had been able to listen
with an untroubled enjoyment to a passage from
the Master. In Paris, it was always in a state
of feverish excitement—with watchful eyes and
fists clenched, ready to pounce upon the inter-
rupters—that we absorbed the new music.

Outside our own country, it appeared, the
cause was already won, and the music of Richard
Wagner already popular. Very slowly we counted
off the different stations, and at length we were

approaching the last one. Our excitement increased. We were overcome by a sort of sacred
terror. We searched among the gods of art for
the one who should appear to us greater than
this one, into whose presence we should so soon
be ushered—for that one in the whole sublime
Olympus of geniuses whom we could prefer to
him, or whom we would rather see, could we be
given the power to choose.

Homer, Æschylus, Dante, Goethe, Beethoven,
we named them all. Even the divine Shakespeare
failed to make us hesitate. To us the name of
Wagner flamed higher, with a more magical lustre.

He was Orpheus and Apollo both, blended to
one lyre. Poet, musician, philosopher—what,
indeed, was he not ? this latest comer.

" He is cubic. He comprises all," said Villiers,
with finality.

" Emmenbrücke," called out the porter.

The last station was passed ; one more half-
hour, and then Lucerne !

Again we rhapsodised, this time seeking new
names for Wagner, eulogistic titles, such as history
has reserved for her greatest men.

" The Eagle of the Righi," " The Swan of

Lucerne "—" The Swan " appeared especially appropriate to us, because of Lohengrin ; but Villiers thought the allusion too ingenuous. " The Swan of Cambrai, the Swan of Lucerne,"— he groped about for a synonym, and finally burst out triumphantly with,

" The Palmiped of Lucerne ! "

An explosion of laughter relieved our nervous tension. But the train whistled, and again our hearts began to beat wildly. Leaning half through the window, dishevelled by the wind, Villiers looked eagerly. It was impossible that anyone could fail to see it—that glorious radiance directly above the city which held such an oracle. Without any doubt, even in the full light of day, a shining star marked, for pious pilgrims, the place of the new Oracle.

We entered the station.

Suddenly, Villiers, pale and with dilated eyes, drew back, and dropped upon the seat, exclaiming,

" The Palmiped ! "

II

It was indeed true !

Standing alone, a big straw hat on his head,

Wagner waited for us on the platform. To be sure, we had never before seen him, but how could anyone fail to recognise him ?

He, who had no idea how we looked, counted upon us to disclose ourselves. Motionless, in full view, he scanned with close attention the stream of arriving people. It was I who hurried toward him, in an effusion of joy which dominated every other emotion.

He included us all in a steady and luminous gaze that reached to the very soul, and then shook hands with us.

After a moment of solemn silence, he smiled and offered me his arm.

" Come," said he to me, " if you do not look for too much magnificence, you will like the Hôtel du Lac. I have engaged rooms for you there."

And, with quick steps, he drew me outside the station.

On the way to the hotel he paused for a moment, and turning on me a steady and serious gaze said, with every appearance of emotion,

" It is a very noble sentiment that brings us together, Madam ! "

The hotel was near the station, and when we

arrived, the Master, after recommending us to the care of the host, turned and said to us with a whimsical air : " Now I am going to prepare myself to receive you, otherwise I should make blunders.   You will come presently to ' Tribschen,' will you not, as soon as you have rested a little ? Come by the lake, that is the most convenient way."

To prepare himself to receive us !

From an upper window we watched him, as with quick steps he went away, saw him cross the old bridge, reach the quay, take a boat.

Without speaking a word, with the same wor-shipping expression upon every face, we followed him with our eyes. . . . Then, when he had quite disappeared, " Quick ! let us dress quickly ! We certainly will not allow him to wait for us."

III

Behold us, in our turn, at the edge of the lake of the " Four Cantons," on the wharf, which shelters a whole fleet of white boats with slackened sails.

What   a   landscape ! What   scenery !—And what a harmonious setting for the picture !

The lake, so pure, so clear that it seems like a mass of blue crystal, a liquid sapphire, is lost to sight between the spurs of the mountains. On one side looms Mount Pilatus, of the purple grey of storm clouds, rugged and bare, outlining against the sky its rocky summit; on the other, verdant Righi undulates, bristling with dark green firs that form a contrast to its bright lawns of tender green. And beyond, dim, cloudy, and unreal, appear the indentations of the Alps.

Choosing a boatman, we call to him, proudly, " To Tribschen."

With a thrust of his boat hook the man launches us from the bank and spreads his sail.

Now it is the city that we see, the old Lucerne with its unequal houses, its many belfries, its unused bastions, spread out above the picturesque little wooden bridge which we had hardly noticed when we crossed it, but which now redoubles the curves of its rustic arches in the blue waters of the lake.

But it is the other horizon only which interests us; that slender promontory over there, which advances at a gentle slope, closing half the passage. Toward that point the breeze gently wafts our

B

rounded sail. There is Tribschen, the domain
of Richard Wagner !

A swan floats upon the lake, majestically
parting the clear water with his snowy breast,
and we imagine we can see between his wings the
golden chain which yoked him to Lohengrin's
little shallop. To our imagination the green
Righi is Mount Salvat; the temple of the Grail
must be concealed there behind the vigilant
trees, and we search at the summit of Pilate
for the giant portal of divine Walhalla.

But we are nearing the promontory; we
can distinguish the slender poplars that stand
erect upon its extreme point, then the trees
and tufted shrubs ranged behind, and there,
through an opening in the branches, we can even
see a gable and a window of the house.

And now we reach the shore. The boat floats
under a little shed built upon piles.

With what deep emotion we set foot upon this
sacred soil !

There is no door, no hedge, no limit to this
garden; the lake, the hills, the forests, the Alps,
the whole world seems a part of it, and even as this
thought appeals to our young enthusiasm, so also

is it true and prophetic, since the world shall, in truth, become the domain of the great one who dwells here.

The earth rises in a gentle slope toward the house, which we see at the other side of a wide lawn. It seems a very simple house, all of gray, long and low under its roof of reddish tiles. In the centre a double flight of seven or eight steps, guarded by an iron balustrade, leads to the drawing-room.

We advance slowly, full of emotion and thoughtful, as at the threshold of a temple. Some one has seen us, undoubtedly, as the Master appears at the door of the drawing-room and descends the steps, a big black Newfoundland bounding by his side.

With an air at once ceremonious and cordial, Wagner bids us enter.

A tall and slender young woman, with a noble and distinguished air, a sweet smile and very blue eyes under her beautiful blond hair, stands in the centre of the drawing-room, surrounded by four little girls, one of them an infant.

"Frau von Bülow, who has kindly come with her children to see me," said the Master, in presenting her.

After shaking hands with us cordially, she tells us the names of her children—Senta, Elisabeth, Isolda, and Eva—who gaze at us with big, wondering eyes.

We recognise in this choice of godmothers, all taken from among the heroines of Wagner, an enthusiasm as great as our own, which drives away all constraint between the charming mother and ourselves.

Then the dogs are presented to us. The big Newfoundland Rouzemouk, or "Russ" familiarly, and Cos, a gray pug belonging to Frau von Bülow.

"My name is Cosima," she tells me, "and my friends at home have formed the very bad habit, which actually gives me chills, of calling me "Cos," so I have given that name to my dog, and since then no one dares call me anything but Cosima!"

So the talk goes on, happy, quick-witted, enthusiastic, the Master almost as gay as the disciples; and we have so much to say!

Wagner speaks French more than moderately well. He speaks it correctly, but in his own way, with a certain freedom and audacity. When he

is unable to find a word to express his exact
thought, or when he believes there is no such
word, he promptly creates one, and always so
clearly, so logically, that one can never fail to
comprehend. He speaks to me of Paris, which
he loves, but where he has suffered much; he
speaks also without bitterness of the great battle
of *Tannhäuser*, concerning which we feel such
mortification for our country. Yet he has gained,
he says, a number of sincere partisans in France
who console him for the defeat. Those who
appreciate him there appreciate him more
thoroughly than his German admirers.

The Frenchman, more nervous, more responsive,
when he does understand, understands at once,
and the warmth of his enthusiasm is very consoling.

The German is more patient and tranquil; he
absorbs conscientiously whatever is presented to
him, but he shows very little feeling; there can be
nothing more frigid, more depressing, than certain
playhouses where the stalls are filled with women
in woollen frocks. "And, in order not to lose
any time at the theatre," cries the Master, in-
dignantly, " they take their knitting with them ! "

Then, also, we look about us with respectful

curiosity, at the interior of the temple, of which the quiet and pervading richness forms a strong contrast to the simple gray of the exterior.

The drawing-room is rather large; it occupies an entire angle of the house, and has windows on two sides. It is bathed in warm and restful shadows between its walls covered with yellow leather traced with arabesques of gold. A thick carpet muffles the footsteps. The velvet draperies of the windows fall in heavy folds and mass themselves upon the floor. A fine portrait of Beethoven holds sway at the end of the grand piano, and faces a mirror which reflects it. Upon two other panels Goethe and Schiller hang facing each other. From the ceiling depends a big bronze lamp.

A large divan of purple damask stands against the wall, and soft easy-chairs and cabinets are grouped here and there.

" Will you come to see my gallery? " asks Wagner, with a smile which mocks the ambitious title. A wide arch connects the drawing-room with a long, narrow room hung in violet velvet, against which the whiteness of small marble statues stands out in soft relief.

They are the heroes of the Master's works :

Tannhäuser touching the strings of his lyre, and singing the passionate song to the glory of Venus. Lohengrin, like an archangel, drawing his sword for the defence of innocence. Tristan, the knight, who believes that he drinks from the goblet of death, and drains instead the cup where sparkles the philtre of love. Walther von der Vogelweide, and the last-born, the youthful and impetuous Siegfried, holding between his fingers the fatal ring.

There are also some tapestries, the gift of King Ludwig of Bavaria, which portray scenes from the Nibelungen. In a niche a gilded Buddha, Chinese incense-burners, chiselled cups—all sorts of rare and precious things. In one corner there are two round table cabinets with covers of glass, which protect a collection of magnificent butterflies with great gold and purple wings.

"This collection of butterflies came from the Paris Exposition," announces the Master, laughing, "and from amid all that great mass of things which owe their existence to the prodigious labours of mankind this is the one thing that an artist finds most to his taste."

Having returned to the drawing-room, our

talk goes on, without constraint. The Master
dazzles us by the charm of his words, his force
and geniality, and, above all, by his incomparable
intellect. Now we begin to feel that it is time
to retire. We disembarked at Tribschen about
five o'clock; it is growing dark and it must be
late, perhaps nearing the dinner-hour, and, above
all, we wish to be discreet and tactful. But at
our first suggestion of going they exclaim with
such an evident cordiality and urge us to stay
with such friendly insistence that in the greatest
content we sit down again.

The children say good-night to everyone, and
go to bed. Lamps are brought, and time passes
most delightfully. But at length—O humiliation !
—our stomachs begin to protest and reproach us
for forgetting them so long. We breakfasted
before leaving Basle this morning, very hastily
and earlier than usual, and it is a long time since
then. Our host has not invited us to dinner,
but since he keeps us on—probably they dine
late at Tribschen.

Toward nine o'clock the door opens; a servant
comes in at last ! But, he brings a tray. It is
only the tea, with the accompaniment of fallacious

dry biscuit. We exchange amused glances. Bah! what does it matter? We will have supper at the hotel. Half-past eleven! Now we really must go. But how? By the lake? Would there still be boats at that hour?

" No, no, by the land. The carriage is in readiness. I will send someone with you." At the other side of the house, upon the threshold of the vestibule, the farewells are prolonged. They make us promise to return the next day, and to come earlier, that we may enjoy the garden and see the country a little. So we roll away through the unknown country and the dark night, ourselves all illuminated with joy. " In Wagner's own carriage! It doesn't seem possible! " exclaims Villiers, patting the cushions. And then we all talk at once, going over every detail of that never-to-be-forgotten day. But the pangs of hunger are tormenting us more and more. What a supper we will have as soon as we reach the Hôtel du Lac! A drowsy boy rouses himself from his pallet bed to open the door for us. " May we have supper? " we request of him. But that isn't his affair; he knows nothing about it. He goes back to bed,

and begins to snore. So we go wandering through
the hotel, trying to open locked doors, ringing
the electric bells again and again. Nothing!
Silence everywhere, and solitude and sleep.   Ah
well, surely we ought to be willing to suffer a
little for the cause that we defend; we ought
not to complain over one day of fasting.
And, since we are unable to avoid it, this
ordeal rather pleases us; it seems fitting and
symbolic; the emptiness of our stomachs permits
us the better to listen to the song of joy in our
hearts, to feel the intoxication of our minds;
and so we go very happily to bed, hoping to see
again in our dreams the sacred promontory over
beyond the blue lake, where we shall return
to-morrow.

IV

And that second day, which dawned with a
beautiful blue sky, how sunny and radiant it
seemed to us! How happy we were and how
full of joyful anticipation! We knew Richard
Wagner and he knew us.

" Come early to-morrow," he had said to us.
That was better and more real than mere polite-

ness. The disciples pleased the Master, of that we were blissfully sure. But, all the same, we must not arrive too soon at Tribschen, and how should we pass the time until the fitting moment arrived? Villiers, who wished to be very smart, went in search of a hairdresser, and fixed his choice upon a certain Monsieur Frey. Installed in the chair, a towel under his chin, his cheeks all covered with soapsuds, the patient, still lost in his dream, recalled a phrase from the letter that Wagner had written me about the *Meister-singer*. "My barber told me the other day, that this part pleased him best of all." So the barbers of Lucerne were Wagnerians? Then he could talk; and with no further hesitation he entered with Monsieur Frey into a dissertation upon the music of the future. The Swiss Figaro did his best to fulfil his part, and the talk being prolonged, Villiers came out of the little shop with a head tightly curled all over like an astrakhan cap. Thus elaborated, he joined us upon the wharf at the edge of the lake, and to forget our impatience we prowled about among the bales and bundles of cordage. My companion hummed a motif from the overture to the *Meistersinger*,

which charmed him more and more. He tried
to prevail upon me to sing at the same time the
second motif, where it mingles with the first.

" How can I, in the open streets ?   They would
throw us both into the lake ! "

" Then let us get out of sight of the passers-by."

So behold us forthwith clambering over joists
and building materials of all kinds, to reach a
deserted corner. Villiers was enchanted with
our humming, which we had to recommence
many times. His quick imagination supplied
all that was lacking ; he fancied he could hear
the whole orchestra. Suddenly he caught sight
of something, and stopped short, his clear blue
eyes very wide open. Staring unwinkingly, he
began to laugh.

" What on earth is that extraordinary word,
' Dampfschifffahrtgesellschaft ? ' "

True enough, there was the word in big letters
on a board painted white, high up between two
posts driven into the soil.

" Six vowels among twenty-three consonants,
and all in one word ! " cried Villiers. " What
can such a word mean ? "

And, uniting our vague notions of German,

we concluded that it signified "Steamship
Company," and that this was the landing-place.
In fact, beyond the poles joined by the plank,
which together formed a sort of door-casing,
there was a wooden staircase which led to a
pontoon. Swans swam about in the blue water
as it lapped against the piles, and the sails,
as white as their wings, bore toward the distant
Eden, toward the promontory which the sun
at that moment covered with a golden mist.
" What time is it ? " Every few moments this
question was asked. At last the time came to
go back to the Hôtel du Lac for dinner. For,
contrary to the French custom, they served a
very hearty dinner there at one o'clock, and if
anything further was desired, a very light supper
at eight ; so finally we understood why, on the
day before, it had seemed to us that they never
dined at Tribschen.

V

Again we arrive at Tribschen. The children
meet us and run on before us to the drawing-
room, where they are waiting for us. With what

sincere cordiality they welcome us ! We are no longer the unknown people of yesterday. Cos hardly barks at all, and Russ, the black Newfoundland, without moving from his place on the steps, slowly sweeps the stone with his plumy tail, to show us his good feeling.

With what pleasure in its restful shade we breathe again the faintly perfumed air of this room. We must sit down and rest a little, they say; but the Master, full of good-humour and high spirits, remains standing. He strives to comprehend the voluble conversation (overflowing with enthusiasm, interspersed with laughter) of Villiers de l'Isle-Adam, and he imagines that if he does not quite get the full meaning, it must be the fault of his imperfect understanding of French. No one of us dares to tell him that in listening to Villiers it is the same for all, that he more often than not twists his language into spirals of unintelligible phrases, through which flash both light and wit. When one knows him well, one sees only these flashes; but the Master does not know him.

So, in order to excuse himself, he relates to us an incident that took place once when he was living at Zurich, through his inability to comprehend French.

An orchestra leader, Alsacian or Belgian, having, in any case, a peculiar accent, was speaking with him of the different ways of directing. He condemned certain habits which he considered hopelessly bad, and emphasised his talk with one phrase which he repeated again and again.

" *C'est comme je vous assure.*"

Wagner heard, " *C'est comme chez vous à Zurich.*"

Irritated, at first, by this rude assertion, he ended by suddenly growing angry, and vehemently defending the Zurich orchestra, which he himself sometimes conducted.

His interlocutor, unable to understand what had caused such anger, was dismayed, excused himself, stammered, and a long time passed before it was made clear.

At the memory of this misunderstanding, Wagner's laugh rang out clear and vibrant, and with all our hearts we laughed with him.

VI

The Master then sat down at the piano, and related to us the poem of *Siegfried*, upon which

he was at that time working. He played the
themes, measure by measure, and declaimed and
sang with such ardour, such vigour, and such a
perfect expression that we seemed actually to
be living the whole drama. The hero, at the
moment of re-forging the sword, strikes a single
blow upon the anvil, and Mime, terror-struck,
falls over backward. Wagner rose and almost
disappeared entirely in the great violet curtains,
in order the better to exemplify the fright of the
gnome. He emerged again laughing, and declared that, not being in any sense a pianist, this
music of the future was too difficult for him.

"I will outline the second act better," said he ;
and he revealed to us the whole bird scene in such
a delightful way that no later execution of it,
anywhere, has quite exalted us to the height of
that vivid first impression.

VII

It is a little cooler now, and we are wandering
through the paths of the garden, with their borders
of tender green. The Master wishes to show
us his domain.

All about us the children run, laughing and

calling to each other with happy voices. Russ bounds on ahead, picks up stones, which he brings back to us with an insinuating air, anxious to draw us into a game, but Wagner is rather grieved over this game. " That is a bad trick I taught him ; now I cannot break him of it, and he damages his teeth against the stones."

The Master walks rapidly ; he guides us toward a high kiosk, where the view, he says, is superb.

In truth, it is a ravishing place. The house seems half buried in a billow of verdure, sheep browse on the slopes of the hills, and below, on the limpid azure of the lake, white sails drift, reflecting the amethyst hues of the high summits. A delicious light bathes in serenity all this wonderful nature.

Richard Wagner, with both hands upon the rustic balustrade of the kiosk, stood erect and silent, with that grave and solemn expression which came to him suddenly when he was touched by any deep emotion.

It was he whom I watched now, and that was an unforgetable instant : his eyes, as blue as the lake, wide open, almost staring, seemed to absorb this picture, which radiated for them a world of thoughts ; this refuge, this exquisite retreat,

c

created by the tenderness of a much-loved friend, who had known how to brave all, and to face the reprobation of the world with head erect, in order to come to the consolation of one to whom she had consecrated herself without reserve, at the time when he was most cruelly pursued by the bitter things of life; this dear solitude, enlivened by the laughter of children, where the blows of destiny could reach him only across a rampart of love—it was with a very tender gratitude that he contemplated it.

He understood that I had followed his thought, for he continued aloud:—

"And yet," said he, "this little corner of earth, so full of memories, does not belong to me; but I intend to buy a small piece of land, just by this side here, so that, later, the children may be able to return here, and at least retain something of this nest of their infancy."

This desire was not realised. The Master, probably, gave up the idea.

VIII

Madam Cosima and our companions rejoined us, and we walked a long time in that limitless

garden. But it was growing late; we could
not abuse our welcome. We wished to take
leave; they exclaimed at that, and we confessed,
with much laughter, our fasting of the day before,
our culpable habit of dining in the evening.
Then the Master showed a real chagrin; he could
not pardon himself for having forgotten that
French customs are different from those of German
Switzerland. We were moved almost to shame
for having provoked such regret, which revealed
to us, however, the keen sensibility and the
sensitive kindness of this much misunderstood
man.

"Beginning with to-morrow," cried he, " a
supper shall be served every evening *here*, and
then you surely must forgive me ! "

IX

At the end of the drawing-room at Tribschen,
to the left in coming from the garden, a heavy
portière, raised by a cord, allowed one a glimpse
of a very small room, which I could not approach
without great emotion. It was the sanctuary,
the Holy of Holies, the work-room of Richard

Wagner! Sombre draperies, a restrained half-light, two walls covered with book-shelves, filled with splendid works: music, poetry, philosophy; a piano of a special design (almost an altar), furnished with drawers and a plane like a table; a single picture, the portrait of Ludwig II., the royal friend, the ministering spirit: "The man who," said Wagner, "seems to have been sent to me from heaven!" What a beautiful, refined face! how the brown tint of the skin and the black hair bring out the splendid clearness of the eyes, of a polar blue, and sparkling with enthusiasm —eyes that seem supernatural.

One and all we love him, this young man; we consider him as our king, our chief and our ally, since he has the same faith as ourselves, and, like us, is in the ranks of the disciples. We were destined for the same mission: to affirm the divinity of a man of genius, to be the mirrors reflecting for him the splendour of his dreams; assuring him of the certainty of his power; soldiers ready to endure insults and blows in his defence, who would gladly fall for his glory. And this king is stronger than we are for the combat; his sceptre bears more weight than our fists.

Sometimes escaping from the court, the royal friend came, alone and incognito, to Tribschen, to celebrate the Master's birthday, or to bring some good tidings. As the house was not large, it was in this little room that they arranged a cot-bed for him. And here he spent several days, very happy, and asking only to be treated as a humble disciple.

Wagner surprised me to-day, on the threshold of this little study, this sanctuary (into which I dared not go), contemplating the piano, the scattered sheets, where the ink was scarcely dry, agitated to the last degree by the human details of the thing that seemed to me so completely superhuman. And I was overcome, almost to suffocation, by hearing suddenly close by my side the voice and the laugh of him who seemed to me, as I looked back through the ages, to stand with Homer, Æschylus, Shakespeare, and to be the one whom I would still have acclaimed as the greatest of all.

" How enthusiastic you are ! " cried he. " You must not be too much so, or your health will suffer." He spoke jestingly, but the kind light in his eyes told me much that his laugh disguised.

X

" This morning," said Wagner to me, " my domestic, Jacob, declared that I must pass the whole day without him, because he was going to Zug."

" ' Zug ! Zug ! ' " That word is on the lips of everyone in Lucerne. We hear it constantly, and I thought it an exclamation, a soothing word, familiar to the Swiss, something like ' Zut.' "

" Not at all. Zug is a little village, very near here."

" And what is there so attractive about it ? "

" Not much, ordinarily ; but evidently you do not know that the Federal shooting-match has begun at Zug. It is the event of all others that develops to its utmost the enthusiasm of all the cantons. A hundred thousand francs in prizes, thirty thousand rifles all together. Seriously, it is curious and interesting, and you ought to see it."

It was in obedience to the Master's counsel, and not without regret at leaving him, that we alighted a few hours later, at the Zug station.

XI

A hen in the midst of her chickens—that is the first impression of the little village of Zug, with its belfry towering up from the midst of the low houses. But what a background it has! The green velvet of the lowest fold of the mountains, which, from there, stretch away, one above another, to the far-away snows of rose and mauve! When one draws near to the little town its aspect changes; now one sees only an ancient fortified gate having in its midst an enormous dial. Large flags wave slowly in the light breeze and the many-coloured banners of the different Swiss cantons hang from every angle of the high roof with its many turrets, which surmounts this gate. Garlands of leaves festoon in many curves, the pointed arch cut in the ancient structure. And when one has passed under the arch, the street stretching away gives one the illusion of a Chinese street, with its houses of unequal height and its perspective of multi-coloured streamers. But one must go by another route to reach the field where the Federal shooting is established. A frightful uproar leads us unerringly to the place. Temporary barracks in the open fields, a crowd of people, gay and solemn, forming a procession. Here and there the picturesque costumes worn by the natives of some cantons still faithful to the old usages.

Bernese with full gathered skirts, half concealed by the apron of silk, of the colour of a pigeon's neck, with the long corsage of black velvet, held by silver chains to the plaited guimpes, and in their hair the great historic pins.

There are peasants from Fribourg clothed in short breeches, with brown jackets, large hats on their heads, and leaning on their ashen staffs. There are even some Tyrolese, drawn from far away by their curiosity, who please the eye by their bright costumes, their narrow tricoloured aprons, their pointed hats of black felt, ornamented with gold braid and worn very low over the forehead.

We have reached the very heart of the hubbub, and it is like that of a frightful battle ; the whistling of thousands of balls, which cut the air without cessation, produces the strangest effect upon the ear. One can imagine oneself wrapped in a network of vibrating iron filaments which weave across and through each other, forming a lattice, and the illusion is so complete that one dares not advance, for fear of injuring these threads. Sheds, divided into compartments and facing in different directions, divide the plain, and in each compartment very busy men hastily load the rifles which they hand to the sharp-shooters, who may be seen from behind taking aim at a far-away target.

Half-unconsciously we allow ourselves to be pushed into one of the boxes, and once there, a Swiss, with the cordial familiarity which prevails in a free country, shouts something into Villiers' ear. He does not hear, but they put a rifle between his hands, and now behold him, in his turn, shouldering and sighting with great care!

What has happened? No one heard the detonation above the uproar, but there is a sudden movement of joyous excitement, and the far-away target, moved by a spring, shakes and salutes the conqueror. Villiers has made a hit! They drag him away; some individuals furnished with enormous trombones appear from somewhere and, forming two lines, make an escort for him. By their puffed-out and crimson cheeks rather

than by sound, one surmises the triumphant
fanfare. They stop at length before a gaily-
painted kiosk, surrounded with glass cases, where
are displayed the prizes for the best marksmen.

There is a framed portrait of Garibaldi, a pair
of gold spectacles, a set of silver, a jewel-box
containing a collection of hundred-sous pieces
with the effigy of Louis Philippe, arranged in
the shape of a star, and many other marvels,
from among which Villiers has only to choose;
but, overcome by laughter, he is unable to
decide. Finally, he unhooks a necklace of
corals and thrusts it in his pocket while someone fastens a commemorative medal to his
hat, where it shines in the midst of a flutter of
ribbons. The victor then wishes to steal away,
but the circle of trombones narrows about him
and urges him toward a pavilion consecrated to
Bacchus, where a commissary of the Fair, mounted
upon a table, solemnly holds out to him the
glorious cup, full of the bitter wine of Sarli, which
he (concealing a grimace of distaste) is obliged
to empty with the best grace possible.

That evening at supper, Wagner was much
interested in the adventure, and in order to do

honour to the skilful marksman, he uncorked
some champágne.

" It is excellent," he said. " My friend Chandon
sent it to me."

XII

One day my companions, having articles to
write, remained at the Hôtel du Lac, and I
arrived alone at Tribschen soon after the two
o'clock dinner, a little fearful of having come,
perhaps, too soon. The clear sky made the
lake very blue and the fresh green of the
banks mirrored itself as usual in the tranquil
water. I disembarked at the point of the promontory by the foot of the garden, under the
little shed which sheltered the wooden steps.

As there was neither door, nor doorkeeper,
nor bell, I arrived without giving any signal,
and, walking slowly, fearing to find my hosts
still at table, I took the least direct route to the
house, through a charming, very shady path
which follows the edge of the lake. It grows
steep very quickly, and the slope which, covered
with bushes, topples down to the water, has the
appearance of a picturesque little precipice, and

nothing could be more lovely to see than the stains of azure made by the lake through the interlacing of the branches. The children have named this corner, where they are forbidden to go alone, for fear of the descents, " The Park of Brigands," and they tell long tales about the adventures which come to pass there after night-fall. At the moment when I came out from the shelter of the trees, the eldest of the little girls saw me and came running, signalling to me not to speak or make any noise. When she reached me, she drew me, without a word, through clumps of trees where I nearly lost my hat, toward a sort of little summer-house of verdure, very near the house, where the coffee had been served. The Master was there, seated on a cane easy-chair, smoking a cigar; Cosima, standing, peeped through the interstices of the bushes, and made me a sign to keep silent: but Wagner, looking at me fiercely, said in a low tone, " What, did you bring all these people ? "

" What people ? "

Cosima called me, by a gesture, near to her, and from there I could see why my hosts were keeping so quietly out of sight. A coach full of tourists had stopped before the steps of the house. A personage clothed entirely in brown holland, against which appeared the black cord of a lorgnette, was interviewing the servant. I thought at first sight that it was a question of some tiresome acquaintance whom they were endeavouring to get rid of as politely as possible; but I soon comprehended that these were foreign tourists, entire strangers, who, with an incredible assurance, insisted upon visiting Richard Wagner. This excursion was doubtless fitted in between the ascension of the Righi and the promenade to the Lion of Lucerne. They insisted with unparalleled impertinence, feigning not to comprehend the assertions of the servant, prolonging the discussion wilfully, while, in the little grove near-by, one dared not breathe, for fear of being discovered. At length Jacob persuaded these intruders that the Master was absent. The carriage was started again amid the creaking of old iron, the gravel of the drive crunched under the wheels, and the vehicle, crowded with green umbrellas, blue veils, and red shawls, went back down the hill.

"At last we are free!" cried the Master, rising.

" How," said I, " could you believe that I
would bring such a rabble here ? "

" You arrived at the same time," said he ;
" but I ought not to have suspected you."

" Nor to have given me that terrible look ! "

" The look was for the tourists," said he, laughing. " I am simply beset by the audacity of
these strangers," added he. " This scene is very
often repeated. The worst of it is that Jacob
is against me. He finds all these people very
distinguished, and cannot understand why I
refuse to see them."

" What a queer situation it would be if one
were to receive them. What would they say,
and what attitude of mind would they reveal ? "

" They relate a curious anecdote of Goethe
with regard to a similar adventure," said Wagner.
" He was so often intruded upon by the curious
in his house in Weimar, that one day, made
impatient by the determination of an unknown
Englishman to force an entrance, he suddenly
ordered his servant to show him in. The Englishman entered. Goethe planted himself erect in
the centre of the room, his arms crossed, his eyes
on the ceiling, motionless like a statue.

"Surprised for the moment, the stranger soon comprehended the situation, and without being in the least disconcerted, he put on his glasses, walked slowly round Goethe, inspected him from head to foot, and went out without saluting. It is difficult to say," concluded the Master, " which of the two showed the keener wit."

XIII

Every evening at eight o'clock—although, honestly ashamed of having been the cause of such a change in the household, we made every effort to prevent it—every evening at eight o'clock, the door of the drawing-room opened and Jacob announced the supper.

The dining-room was rather small and narrow, and was nearly filled by the oblong table, at one end of which Wagner took his place.

To the supper, consisting of cold meats, salad, cakes and fruit, the Master loved to add some of the champagne of his friend Chandon, and this, he said, we could drink without hesitation because his French admirer had presented him with more than he could use.

Wagner enjoyed this supper and declared that

he could not understand why he had not instituted
it long before.

"We never thought of it," said he.   "It is
an incredible oversight not to have thought of
a thing so agreeable, even indispensable!   In
future, it shall always be served, and we shall
bless the reform that was brought about by your
fasting of the first evening."

We lingered at table, talking.   The Master's
words, now violent and impassioned, now joyous,
but always sincere, made an intense, almost
a magnetic impression upon us.   We passed
through all the phases that they described—
enthusiasm, indignation, despair.   Each circum-
stance that he recalled of his life, so full of vexations, " *les misérabilités*," as he said, he seemed
to live over again, and we also endured with
him all the heart-breaks and the pangs.   Yet,
if he saw us becoming too deeply moved, in order
that we might recover ourselves, he would give
expression, without any change of voice, to some
irresistible bit of fun, and end by making us shout
with laughter.

The pug-dog, " Cos," having a slight irritation
of the skin, was on a diet, and meat had been

forbidden him. If, unable to resist his urgent
pleadings, one of the company stealthily gave
him a little morsel, Wagner stopped abruptly
in whatever he was saying, and emphatically
repeated the doctor's orders. It was wonderful,
that considerate thoughtfulness, in which nothing
escaped him; and it revealed to us the infinite
goodness, the boundless altruism of that great
man, with his overwhelming personality.

XIV

Alas! we were none of us capitalists. This
pious pilgrimage to the temple of genius and our
glorious sojourn there must be paid for, and the
money must be earned.

We had undertaken to send to the different
journals exhaustive accounts of the Munich Exposition, with letters of travel, and above all,
items of news about Richard Wagner, who at
that time was the subject of many discussions
and disputes. Living, as he did, in strict seclusion,
he aroused the curiosity of the people to the
highest point.

Not without misgivings, I had written an
D

article for *Le Rappel*, entitled " Richard Wagner at Home."

I did not enlarge upon this to the Master himself, and I sincerely hoped he would never hear of it ; but someone, believing it would please him, sent him the article.

He was angry.

" A discord already ! " he cried. Then he declared to Cosima that his house and all things relating to his private life, including the dogs, were to him like the mysterious jewel of his destiny, and that he experienced actual terror at seeing them mentioned in the papers.

Cosima did her utmost to excuse and defend me, and the Master was appeased. But a Lucerne leaflet, the *Journal des Étrangers*, took upon itself to reprint the article, thereby drawing to the vicinity of Tribschen a swarm of boats filled with inquisitive observers, and Wagner was freshly annoyed. He felt a real chagrin, he said, because he could not endure such things from his friends, and he wished to consider us his friends. At length, having given him my promise not to repeat the offence, he pardoned it ; and a few days later, in order to amuse me, he gave me the

following letter—to read and then destroy—
which had made them laugh heartily, and which
a lady of Thonon had been inspired to write by
my article, " Richard Wagner at Home."

" My dear Sir,

" Pray pardon me for writing to you in this way,
but I have just seen, in a newspaper, an article
about you, and it is with the deepest emotion
that I have read all the eulogies it contains, for,
my dear Sir, I see that you, also, have passed
through evil days. Being myself, at the present
time, in the same unfortunate position, I can the
more deeply sympathise with you, my dear Sir.

" I was brought up amid the greatest luxury,
and was the object of every care and consideration.
Unhappily for me, family misfortunes and reverses
came upon me, and we lost all. Those who used
to call themselves our friends no longer know us.

" Thank God, I have had the best possible
education. I am passionately fond of music,
but, alas ! since our misfortunes, I have not
touched a piano, and the fact that I have not the
means to procure one is an immense deprivation
and a real grief to me.

" Why am I not close to you, my dear Sir !

In that case, I feel sure that you would not
refuse me admission to your house, and a place
at your piano.

" As for me, I have five children, and I have
not the means for a home, but if I could be near
you, my dear Sir, it seems to me that I should be
happy.

" I should be indifferent to all other privations,
if I were able to cultivate the art which is so dear
to me.

" I foresee your astonishment, my dear Sir,
when you read my letter ; but if I could only see
you, you would no longer be surprised. I know
beforehand that your house will be mine, and
your piano will be mine. . . ."

" Your piano will be mine. . . ." That phrase
remained famous for a long time at Tribschen.

XV

One day, having landed at Tribschen, as I
reached the house, I heard through the wide-open
windows of the drawing-room, mingling with the
light voices and laughter of the children, the sound
of a curious melody. What could be happening ?
Not wishing to interrupt, I advanced very care-

fully in order not to be heard on the gravelled path, and, having climbed the steps, I saw a delightful picture.

In the centre of the room, the four little girls, the youngest of whom was hardly three, were dancing. Wagner, at the piano, provided the music. The smallest child laughed with delight, revealing all her little new teeth, as she strove to follow the steps of the older ones. Her tiny feet tapped the floor vigorously, out of time with the rhythm which the player, himself laughing and exclaiming as much as the dancers, nevertheless marked with much force. When they grew tired of dancing, I went in.

" Oh, did you see ? " cried Senta, running toward me. " That is the Tailors' Quadrille. Papa composed it for us."

" The Tailors' Quadrille." Music of Richard Wagner ! If one could only remember that music now ! If one could only know, at least, that it is written down and preserved ! As for me, I seem to hear it again when I recall that scene, which I remember in every detail, and which is, even to-day, as vivid and living as it is exquisite !

XVI

Villiers had some very singular traits of character
to which his old friends paid no attention, but
which never failed to astonish those who knew
him but slightly and had never been forewarned.
He experienced, on occasions, a sort of nervous
terror which he did not even attempt to resist.

For instance, one day as he was talking with
some one at a street corner, he received in his
eye an infinitesimal spatter of saliva. Seized
with a sudden panic, Villiers darted away from
his amazed interlocutor, and with all speed made
for the nearest pharmacy.

His vivid imagination had instantly foreseen
all the possibilities of calamity, by this venomous
drop he felt himself inoculated with the most
baleful maladies. He saw himself condemned,
lost ! To quiet him, the chemist with great haste
had made a point of bathing his eye in all sorts
of supposedly powerful lotions.

One afternoon at Tribschen, Villiers was playing with the children ; tossing a ball, which, to
their great glee, he sent very high in the air.
Russ, the Newfoundland, bounding from place

to place and barking, did his best to join in the sport.

But once, as he gave a strong impetus to the ball, Villiers' recoiling fist struck a sharp blow on the dog's jowl, drawing from him a reproachful whine. Villiers grew pale as he examined his hand, and found a red mark where the dog's tooth had lightly scratched the skin; then, with one haggard look at us, he turned and fled, running as only he could run.

" What is the matter? Where is he going? " cried Wagner in dismay.

Some answer had to be made.

" Oh, it is nothing. He struck his hand against the teeth of poor Russ, and grazed the skin."

" Yes, I know; but it did not bleed. Is that why he grew so pale? "

" A brain like his receives quick suggestions; in the flash of an eye his thoughts fly to the very limit of possible consequences. Villiers doubtless believes himself in danger of hydrophobia, and as in such case delay adds to the danger, he is running as fast as he can to Lucerne, to have the wound cauterised."

" But there is no wound."

Wagner received an unpleasant impression. He was clearly disturbed by Villiers, whose conversation he found it so difficult to understand, and whose character he could not comprehend.

But it was best to laugh it off. The involuntary culprit, good old Russ, was in perfect health, and there could not be any danger.

When Villiers, feeling rather sheepish, returned to Tribschen on the following day, Wagner, as soon as he saw him in the distance, made a pretence of extreme terror, and exclaimed,

" He is mad ! He is mad ! "

And as Villiers with a wry smile approached nearer to him, he broke into a run, crying out, " Do not bite me ! " Then, as if to escape from the danger, he climbed with extraordinary agility to the very top of a pine-tree.

XVII

The Master asked me if I knew the Military March he had dedicated to the King of Bavaria. He had on his piano a copy of this piece, arranged for four hands.

" Let us play it," said he. " But I warn you that I play the piano very badly."

What of my playing, then! But I felt that I must not disclose my weakness, that, at any cost, this wonderful, rare moment must be enshrined in my memory :—to have played a duet with Richard Wagner, if it were only a few bars !

He took the upper part, and as the bass is more difficult for me, that made the matter worse. But I seated myself courageously, mentally determined to make every effort of which I was capable.

We began to play, without stumbling. I felt as though I were a somnambulist walking on a narrow ledge, and I seemed to have been doing so for a very long time.

But at last, on the third page, Wagner himself hesitated and then stopped, declaring that part too difficult.

" How well you keep the time ! " he exclaimed. And then he complimented me upon my way of rolling the *tremolos*. That particular merit was most assuredly brought to light by the emotion of the moment, as I had never known of it before.

My *tremolo*, moreover, remained celebrated at Tribschen—and even at Wahnfried—for I have

lived upon my reputation, and, despite all solicita-
tions, I have never risked attempting it again.

Wagner made me a present of that copy of the
Cavalry March which I had so anxiously deciphered, and he wrote above the first line :

"À Cheval !   À Quatre Mains."

XVIII

" I wish to say to you," announced the Master,
one day as we arrived, " that you are invited
by me to make an excursion into a very interesting
corner of Switzerland — the country of William
Tell. The trip is all planned, and everything is
arranged."

Again we were rather embarrassed, and endeavoured to protest. But Madam Cosima made
signs to me, and, coming nearer, said in a low
voice :

" Do not refuse : he would be angry. And let
him manage it all ; let him take the lead, if you
do not wish to grieve him."

" The weather is beautiful," continued Wagner.
" We ought not to wait. If it is convenient to
you, let us start to-morrow."

" Joyfully, Master."

" Then that is agreed upon. We shall begin
the journey by coach, and will call for you at the
Hôtel du Lac."

" At what hour ? "

" Ah ! as to that, it must be early in the morning
in order to avoid the great heat. Be ready at
half-past five."

" Half-past five. We shall be ready."

The next day, before day in fact, two carriages
stopped before the Hôtel du Lac. Wagner was
alone in one : Madam Cosima and her daughter
Senta occupied the other.

We descended hurriedly, all ready to go, if
still a little sleepy. Villiers, very much flurried,
instead of going directly to the carriage, tried to
get into the little shop of Monsieur Frey, close at
hand ; but the amiable hairdresser was not yet
awake, and his disappointed client was forced to
go without being curled. He went with me in
Wagner's carriage, which took the lead, and the
expedition started on its way.

What roads we travelled, what landscapes un-
folded before us during that radiant and never-
to-be-forgotten morning, I should be quite unable

to relate, for I avow that I saw nothing! When one has gazed at the sun, for a long time one sees nothing more than a flame which comes between the eyes and all other things. So it was with me; the face of the Master masked all Nature, so that I saw only that. I remember very well that the slanting rays of the rising sun enveloped Wagner, and cast a light on his under-lip; this light sparkled at every inflexion, and his words seemed like stars.

I had questioned him with regard to Mendelssohn: the works of Mendelssohn had a great charm for me, which endured in spite of my Wagnerian exclusiveness, a fact of which I was a little ashamed.

" Mendelssohn is a great landscape-painter," said he to me, " and his palette has a richness that is unequalled. No one else transposes the external beauty of things into music as he does. The Cave of Fingal, among others, is an admirable picture. He is able, conscientious, and clever. Yet, in spite of all these gifts, he fails to move us to the depths of the soul : it is as if he painted only the appearance of sentiment, and not the sentiment itself."

Before noon we expected to reach an inn, where we should try to get luncheon, or rather, the German dinner. At that point the coaches were to be abandoned, and the journey would be continued by steamboat.

For a long time we skirted the edge of a lake, very blue between its green banks—that is all I remember about it; then stopped in front of a commonplace little house by the side of the road. Where this was I do not know. A recent study of Baedeker makes me suppose that it was at a place called Brunnen.

On the other side of the road was the lake, and the landing-place for the boats was almost in front of the house.

There was nothing to indicate that it was an inn, but the Master knew the people, and while we went upstairs to a room on the first floor, furnished only with a round table, some chairs, and an old piano, he conferred with the pro-prietor and arranged the *menu*. He returned to us triumphant, and cried:

" We shall have ' un druide ' of ancient Gaul ! "

The meaning of this terrible pun did not strike us at first, but we laughed immoderately when

we found that it was a question of " une truite "
(a trout) !

Two windows of the little room that we were
in faced the lake, a third, a side window, was
open and overlooked the court, where a blacksmith
was at work. Wagner listened to the ringing
stroke of the hammer on the anvil. Suddenly
he opened the piano and began to play the *motif*
of Siegfried forging the sword. At the measure
where the blade is struck he stopped, and it was
the blacksmith who, striking the iron with an
astonishing precision, unconsciously completed
the theme.

" You see," said the Master, " how well I have
calculated the time, and how exactly the blow falls."

But " *le druide* " made his entrance, and we
proceeded to render him the honours that he
merited.

XIX

Wagner was an admirable organiser. Just as
the coffee was finished and the cigarettes smoked,
we heard the whistle of the steamboat, and had only
to cross the road and go aboard. What is there to
tell about this voyage, except that there are some

moments in life when all nature is illuminated
by the light that you carry within yourself;
when the air seems more limpid, the sky more
luminous, the water more transparent; when all
vibrates harmoniously throughout the scene which
envelops your joy.

Certain it is that there was never for me such
a blue lake between such fresh hills, and yet I
did not see them. The face of the Master, his
beaming eyes, where blended the most beautiful
shades of sapphire—that was what I saw, and I
said to Madam Cosima, who thought quite as I
did,—

" Now, at last, I comprehend that happiness
of paradise, so extolled by believers, the seeing
of the Gods face to face ! "

The setting sun illumined a beatified sky
when the boat stopped at the last station. The
lake appeared to end there, and I believe the
little port where we disembarked was called Treib,
and from there one ascended to Seelisberg.

I was altogether unacquainted with the previous
life of Richard Wagner; I knew nothing of his
political exile or of his long sojourn in this country
where he was leading us : I had no idea of the

ordeals he had passed through, of the heart-breaks which had preceded the consoling lull of the present hour, this happy time of renewed inspiration, during which I had the good fortune to find him so full of joy, of energy, and of serenity.

I was, therefore, very much surprised, delightfully surprised, by the scene which followed his landing. Before he put his foot on shore he had been recognised. Very soon a crowd assembled : boatmen, residents, attendants, all hurried toward him, and with wonderful enthusiasm acclaimed Richard Wagner, pressing his hands, kissing his garments with a sort of adoration. The Master thanked them laughing, but with wet eyes. He drew us quickly away from the crowd.

" These good people," said he, " they have not forgotten me yet."

Then he told us how much this land of exile had meant to him.

" I arrived here like a criminal driven out of his country, knowing not where to find refuge. This is the very village to which I came. And that first night when, sad and disheartened, I made ready to sleep in a strange room, a chorus of men, accompanied by harps and brass instru-

ments, broke forth under my window. Dressing
again quickly, I opened the shutters, and saw on
the lake several boats hung with lanterns, and
filled with men who sang. Can you imagine my
emotion in listening to them? For they sang
my music, fragments from my operas! I could
hardly believe my ears. How could it happen
that while I was fleeing from one country which
hated me, here, in this out-of-the-way village,
I was loved; they knew my works, and welcomed
me like this? I have lived a long time among
these honest Swiss people, and I am deeply grateful to them, because at the moment of my greatest
despair they gave me back faith and hope."

Wagner spoke with feeling, and his voice was
serious; but his laugh rang clearly as he added:

" And that is why you will have bad beds to-
night, and an indifferent supper. For I know
you would not have me take you to any other
inn than this one from which I carried away such
a memory."

XX

The inn was, indeed, badly kept, but delightfully situated, at the base of the mountains and

E

close to the margin of another lake, which the setting sun transformed into a basin of gold.

When our rooms had been given us and supper ordered, Wagner proposed that we should go by boat to the place where a stream gushes out from the rock, and is supposed to possess all sorts of virtues, among others that of granting forgetfulness to whomsoever shall drink of its waters.

The inn-keeper himself rigged up his boat for us, and offered to take us there. With one shove of his boat-hook he launched it upon the luminous surface, which shivered and darkened into blue shadows.

Wagner began to sing, since we were now in the land of William Tell,

> " Accours dans ma nacelle,
> Timide jouvencelle. . . . "

But we responded with themes from *The Flying Dutchman*, and after that, *Lohengrin*. Then the Master joined in, and started the song of the Ship-boy from *Tristan*. All the *motifs* of the first and third Acts which have to do with a ship were passed in review; *The Rhinegold* also had its turn, and at last Wagner cried :

" We have exhausted all my aquatic music ! "

The mountains made an almost sheer descent to the lake. We reached the spring that spouts from the rock. Madam Cosima wished to taste this water, but I declared that I would not drink, lest I should lose the memory of the wonderful journey.

The twilight lowered; gradually everything was obscured, and we sailed under the deepening shadows. Wagner thought it would be more prudent not to leave the boat, but to return to the inn, where supper awaited us.

XXI

After supper, silent and thoughtful, seated about the Master on the terrace of the inn, we gave ourselves up to the grave and restful influences of the night, so quickly fallen between those high mountains which enclosed us. The lake was invisible save for a few faint reflections.

But now a soft radiance stole over the sky. Little by little the outlines of the mountains stood out, very sombre against the lighter background; and, gradually, the magnificent spectacle of a rising moon unrolled before our eyes.

The diffused light increased and concentrated, surging higher and higher; the prelude to *Lohengrin* sang itself in our hearts, and when, at last, the full moon emerged, lifted above the highest summit, it was for us the Grail shining upon the altar, before the Master of the Grail.

XXII

"Allons, Enfants de la Patrie!
Le jour de gloire est arrivé!"

So sang Wagner from the *Marseillaise* at the top of his voice, as he beat a tattoo on the door of my bedroom to awaken me; and he passed on to each door, beating the same refrain.

We should have to dress very quickly, as we must climb a mountain and reach the summit before noon, if we wished to breakfast there.

This mountain was called the Axenstein. We commenced the ascent on foot, on a lovely day, under a sunshine already warm. The way at the beginning was charming, and mounted very slowly between trees and bushes, like a garden path.

Senta ran on before and gathered little wild flowers; very soon she gave a cry of joy. She

had just discovered some strawberries. Surely
enough, there were wild strawberries reddening
under the leaves here and there. We also, Madam
Cosima and I, were intent upon finding them;
but Wagner, already far in advance, called out
to us not to linger, and so, by a path grown more
rugged and without any shade, we hurried on.
My companion seemed very tired and almost
fainting. I made her sit down on a grassy hillock,
and after inhaling some salts, she recovered herself
quickly.

"Do not speak of it. Above all, do not let
the Master know," she said. Then she told
me that she had been more or less ailing and
feeble since the birth of Siegfried, her son, whom
she had not yet presented to me.

"Wagner, who is indefatigable, always supposes
that one has strength to follow him, and would
be inconsolable if he were to know that he is mistaken. That is why it is necessary to triumph over
weakness and continue the ascent."

XXIII

The hotel was one of those sumptuous and
comfortable structures which are to be found all

over Switzerland, with the domestic in a dress
coat, whose presence gives you a shock of disappointment when he receives you with a smile,
at the moment when you reach a summit which
you had imagined to be almost inaccessible.
The view was, undoubtedly, very wonderful,
since we had been obliged to mount so high in
order to enjoy it, but I am ashamed to say that
I have not retained any memory of it. The
Master was exuberantly gay : again he found
old acquaintances, old servants, among the re-
tainers of the hotel, with whom he joked familiarly,
which annoyed Madam Cosima very much, as she
could have wished him to be more reserved, more
Olympian.

In the corner that had been selected for us in
the immense dining-room, the dinner, lubricated
with champagne, was hilarious and particularly
delicious. In honour of Wagner, the proprietress
of the hotel, whose outline insistently suggested
the fairy Carabosse, had herself superintended its
preparation. We prolonged it until a late hour,
as it was the last day of the excursion : on the
following day we should have to descend again,
to take the steamboat and return to Lucerne.

It was only after the return that Wagner confessed that he had been indisposed all through
the journey ; but he had taken great care not to
let us perceive it, in order not to spoil our pleasure.

XXIV

For several days we had noticed that they
treated us with extraordinary respect at the
Hôtel du Lac. If we rang, they ran to answer
our call before the bell had stopped vibrating,
owing to the fact that the servants always remained
in the corridor, to take our orders the more quickly.
At table, because we had once complimented the
master of the hotel on a particularly delicious
dish of spinach, they now served us spinach more
and more delicious at every meal. When we left
our rooms stealthy and curious eyes looked at
us through half-open doors along the passage.
They saluted us with an obsequiousness most
unusual in free Switzerland. They almost appeared to form in line as we passed, and already
in the city it was evident that our presence
created a strange excitement. Was it because
they knew us to be friends of Richard Wagner,
and because the jealously-guarded retreat in

which he lived was open for us? Certainly no
glory appeared to us more enviable, and our just
pride equalled our joy. But why should we
cause such a commotion amid the placid population of Lucerne? Could it be that we were
surrounded by a luminous mist, visible to less
fortunate mortals?

When we set sail for the little cape of Tribschen,
clouds of other sails, with an appearance of un-
concern, put out from the banks to escort us from
afar, and as long as we remained at the home of
our illustrious host, they increased all about the
edges of the grounds, drawing as near as possible.

We had told the Master and Madam Cosima
about this, and they were as puzzled as we were.
Sometimes we went into the garden, to look
through the trees at all those boats, full of
tourists, which waited there so stubbornly with
that incomprehensible air of expectation.

This mysterious thing finally explained itself.
Madam Cosima, in going to Lucerne one day to
take Senta for her piano lesson, met the owner
of Tribschen, and he himself, without being asked,
gave the keyword of the enigma.

" Everyone in Lucerne knows," said he, " that

the King, Ludwig II. of Bavaria, is here *incognito*. The Chief of Police said to me, ' I have an unerring scent, and I know that he is there.' "

Everyone knew that the King had had his hair dressed at the shop of M. Frey, and that he had honoured the fortunate barber with a conversation upon Wagner; that at the Zug rifle-match he had condescended to compete, and victoriously, and that he had made with the Master an excursion to the Axenstein. . . .

The piano-teacher knew the story, but she also told Cosima something more. Adelina Patti had been at Tribschen for the last fifteen days. The King had brought her there, so that she might study a part, which it would be her duty to create in the next work of Wagner. That was why all the boatmen received orders to draw as near as possible to the Master's house, in order that the tourists might perhaps catch, on the wing, a few notes of the *diva*. It was Villiers de l'Isle-Adam whom they had taken for the King of Bavaria, and it was in my person that the Lucerne imagination had recognised Madam Patti. One of our companions was, beyond any doubt, the blond Count de Taxis.

" You see," Wagner said to us, " that you have not only touched two hearts which, through being armed so long against human malice, have become almost callous, but you have also put in a flutter the usually very apathetic brains of the inhabitants of Lucerne ! "

All was very clear, now that we understood it; but now we must proceed to undeceive these firmly convinced people. All our denials, like the hammer that strikes upon the nail, only served to deepen the certainty of their minds. It only remained to amuse ourselves with this short royalty. We profited by it to the extent of being served like princes at the Hôtel du Lac.

XXV

One day I had been invited to Tribschen for the two o'clock dinner. Over the lake, as usual, a boatman rowed me to the point of the promontory, and I passed through the garden and up to the house without meeting anyone. The French windows of the drawing-room were wide-open, and as I reached the threshold I heard soft harmonies that came from the little sanctuary where the Master worked. Hardly daring to breathe, I slipped into the nearest chair. I was greatly moved, troubled, even frightened, for was it not a presumption, almost a sacrilege, to surprise in this way the sacred mystery? Yet, what rare good fortune was mine, to hear Wagner composing! Perfectly quiet, hardly moving an eyelash, I listened intently. Incomparably sweet appeared to me the sounds I heard. A very slow progression of chords, which seemed to be drawn from a harp rather than a piano : a strange, remote harmony, mysterious and supernatural. I discovered, later, that it was the first sketch of the Invocation to Erda by Wotan, in the Third Act of *Siegfried*, where the goddess ascends from the depths of the earth, with closed eyes and draperies wet with dew. . . .

After a few moments, silence fell, and Wagner soon appeared between the silken folds of the parted curtains.

His face, with its aureole of silvered hair, was calm, and still more luminous than usual were the rays that beamed from his large eyes.

He saw me sitting rigid on my chair.

" Ah ! " he said, " are you there ? As quiet as an image ! I have not heard a sound."

" Imagine, then, O Master, what terror and what ecstasy I have felt, to surprise Deity in the act of creating."

" I have told you before that you must not be so enthusiastic," he exclaimed laughingly. " It is bad for the health."

" Oh ! no ; on the contrary, it makes one doubly alive."

" Well, I have been good too. Come and see how well I have worked."

A perfume of white-rose extract pervaded the little chapel. A restful light, subdued by the surrounding verdure, illumined it ; two or three rays fell on the gilded backs of the books, and the royal friend in his golden frame seemed to follow one with the magic glance of his polar blue eyes.

There was no disorder on the piano-desk. Several large sheets of music-paper, nearly covered with writing, concealed here and there the dark woodwork. The part which the Master had just composed was written in pencil, in very fine, close writing.

" I copy with the pen," he said. " I like to have it very clear. When I cannot decipher it, I am furious."

I read at the top of a re-copied page,

"Siegfried. Third Act."

" As a matter of fact," exclaimed Wagner, " I ought to rewrite from nearly two pages back, because I have smudged it."

And he showed me where, on the right side of the leaf, three bars were scratched out. They had been erased angrily, by three slurs, very heavily marked and resembling a series of *e*'s and *l*'s.

" What will become of this precious paper, then ? " I asked.

" Would you like it ? " replied the Master, divining my covetousness.

" Oh ! yes."

Then, taking his pen, he dated it on the margin at the top of the page, " From Tribschen."

It is the wonderful prelude from the Third Act of *Siegfried,* before the Invocation to Erda. It is sketched in three lines, with instrumental indications, and a few pencilled alterations. I did not yet know all the beauty contained in those two pages, the possession of which filled me with joy.

The bell for *déjeuner* sounded, and I heard the laughter of the children. They were looking for us. Wagner gallantly offered me his arm to escort me to the dining-room.

XXVI

At table, Wagner told us about a very interesting French leaflet which he had once read in Paris, and which he had never been able to find again. It was a history of Bluebeard, with the traditional slaying of his wives and the forbidden chamber; but in this account the last-threatened victim was not saved in the usual way, by her brothers. No less a person than Jeanne d'Arc came to deliver her and punish the criminal.

"I remember," said the Master, "that there were illustrations. As a matter of fact, it was a cheap edition, printed in two columns. I have no idea how this pamphlet came into my hands, nor how it was lost, but I have never forgotten it. That bringing together of Jeanne d'Arc and Bluebeard impressed me very much. The monstrous Gilles de Retz, who may have served as a model for the legendary type of Bluebeard,

was a contemporary of *La Pucelle*, and the hypo-
thesis of that heroine's coming to the aid of
innocence and chastising the guilty is very
curious. I should be glad if I could find that
funny little leaflet again."

(Alas ! it was not to be found, in spite of all
researches.)

Toward the middle of the dinner, Wagner,
who had been silent for a little time, asked our
permission to go and note down an idea which
had crossed his mind, and which he feared he
might forget, *à propos* of the study of Beethoven
upon which he was then at work.

He went up to his bedroom to write these few
sentences, and I concluded from that fact that
the Master did not write his volumes of prose in
the same holy place where he composed his music.

XXVII

In the " gallery," beside the marble statue
of Tristan, stood a photograph framed in velvet
which reproduced the features of a handsome,
athletic young man, with an intensely ardent
expression. I was very curious about this portrait,

which always attracted my attention and held it irresistibly. One day I questioned the Master.

" Who is that young man ? "

I saw him grow pale ; his eyes filled with tears, and with a repressed sigh, he murmured,

" My poor Schnorr ! "

Madam Cosima signed to me not to say anything more, and as soon as it was possible, she told me all about it.

" It is a photograph of Schnorr von Karolsfeld, ' the hero of song,' as Wagner called him— suddenly cut off by Death in the very fulness of triumphant life. Five years have passed since then, but the Master cannot console himself for the loss of this friend, this disciple, this marvellous interpreter of his work. He never thinks of him without a pang and, above all, he dreads to speak of him."

" Schnorr was the son of a celebrated painter, and had received a fine education. He was very gifted in all the arts, and by reason of one more rare and wonderful gift, that of an incomparable voice, he had been drawn toward music and the stage. From his first acquaintance with the works of Richard Wagner, Schnorr had comprehended and profoundly loved them. Despite the increasing celebrity of the young artist, the Master for a long time rather dreaded to see him because of what he had heard of his too great corpulence : he feared that this physical imperfection might prejudice and render him unjust to all his other qualities. So, because he was little skilled in concealing his impressions, he avoided being brought in contact with the interpreter of his works. It was, therefore, with great secrecy that he went one evening to Karlsrühe (where Schnorr was engaged for a representation of *Lohengrin*) and entered the theatre without being recognised.

" Later, the Master himself told the story of that wonderful evening.

" ' All my apprehensions very soon disappeared. It is true that the first appearance of the Knight of the Swan as he drew near to the shore, looking like a young Hercules, made a rather strange impression upon me, but this disappeared as the hero advanced. The peculiar charm of the messenger from God works instantly. Of this character one did not ask, " Who is he ? " but said, " It is he."

F

" 'Truly, this sudden and profound impression
can only be compared to a kind of enchantment.
I remember having felt this very decidedly when
I was a boy, concerning the great Schroeder-
Devrient. I have never experienced it since
so strongly, so decisively as at the entrance of
Ludwig Schnorr in *Lohengrin*. While I recognised,
in the course of his interpretation, that in many
ways his understanding and rendering of my
work had not yet attained maturity, yet even in
that I saw the charm of a youthful purity still
untouched, of a virgin soil that promised to bring
forth flowers of great artistic perfection. The
fervour, the tender exaltation that burned in the
marvellously love-filled eyes of this very young
man, made me feel vaguely how ill-omened might
be the fire by which they were enkindled. Very
soon I discovered in him a being who, by the very
reason of his unlimited gifts, inspired in me a
tragic pity.'

" The meeting between the Master and the
disciple was cordial and touching. And what a
glad surprise for the creator of *Tristan and Isolde*,
to discover that Schnorr, filled with enthusiasm
for this work, reputed to be unsingable, had made

himself thoroughly acquainted with it, and knew the *rôle* of Tristan from one end to the other! Nevertheless, he had hesitated to sing it, all because of a passage in the Third Act. He did not quite comprehend what ought to be the musical expression of this especial passage, which he judged to be one of the highest importance.

" This unselfish scruple gave Wagner one of the vivid surprises of his life. Could it be possible that a tenor acclaimed by all should have so little vanity and be so nobly conscious of his artistic mission ? Could he so mistrust himself and, in spite of his experience and his pre-eminence, believe himself incapable of interpreting a *rôle* because he did not entirely comprehend the exact expression of a single passage in so complicated a work ? And the idea of cutting out this phrase, the first that would have occurred to any other singer, had not even suggested itself to this rare soul.

" The passage in question, in the Third Act of *Tristan*, runs as follows :

> ' Aus Vaters Noth und Mutter Weh,
> Aus Liebes-thränen eh' und je,
> Aus Lachen und Weinen, Wonnen und Wunden,
> Hab' ich des Trankes Gifte gefunden !

Den ich gebraut, der mir geflossen,
Den Wonne Schlürfend je ich genossen,
Verflucht sei furchtbarer Trank,
Verflucht wer dich gebraut !'

" It is a climax in that delirious raving of Tristan separated from Isolde, that frenzied longing which only found relief in unconsciousness.

" The Master explained certain things to Schnorr; especially he gave him the idea of a wider, less rapid, movement, which suddenly cleared all that had been obscure to the young artist, who showed at once that he had understood by interpreting the passage in a way that was without a fault.

" ' Who can measure the extent of the hopes that thrilled me at the moment when such a singer came into my life ! '

" Such was Wagner's cry of gratitude. And from that day he made every effort to obtain a representation of *Tristan*, with the co-operation of Schnorr.

" There were still many years before this beautiful dream was realised, and then it came to pass through the intervention of the royal friend, the archangel so miraculously sent, whose flaming sword reduced all obstacles to ashes and made free the path toward the ideal.

"These first representations of *Tristan* at Munich were among the most memorable of artistic events. Those who had the good fortune to take part in them preserved a splendid memory and a nostalgic longing. So great a work produced with such perfection and, during the rehearsals, such complete harmony between the Master and the interpreter!

"To quote the Master's own words:

"'The clumsiest of would-be musicians, singer or instrumentalist, would never have accepted from me such minute instructions as did that hero of song, who, without effort, arrived at such a mastery. Any indication of mine upon which I laid the slightest stress he accepted and acted on with cheerful promptness, grasping the reason for it at once, and in such a way that I should have felt that I had failed in my duty if, through fear of wounding his feelings, I had withheld my suggestion, however minute it might be. The reason for this disposition on the part of my friend is that the ideal comprehension of my work had come to him quite spontaneously; he absorbed my ideas so naturally that not the slenderest thread of the spiritual woof, not the slightest

allusion to the most obscure harmonies escaped
him; he felt them all in a very subtle way.'

" ' So nothing remained for him but to select as
rigorously as possible the technical methods of
expression for the singer, the musician, and the
actor that would best secure a perfect harmony
between the personal gifts of the artist in their
particular effect and the ideal object of the
interpretation. All who were present at those
studies will be able to testify that they never
before witnessed such an amicable and artistic
understanding. Having explained to him the
one passage which he had not comprehended
I never had any further talk with Schnorr about
the Third Act of *Tristan*. After paying the
closest attention to the rehearsals of the First
and Second Acts, when the Third Act commenced
I involuntarily turned away from the hero,
wounded unto death, and, sitting motionless
upon my chair with my eyes half-closed, became
completely absorbed in the music. As I never
turned toward him during this tremendous scene
even at his most impassioned utterances, Schnorr
appeared to have been abashed by my long
silence and seeming indifference; but when,

after the malediction of love, I finally got up and
going unsteadily to this wonderful friend, who
still remained prostrate on his couch, I leaned
over him and, embracing him vehemently, said
to him in a subdued voice that I had no criticism
to make, that from this time forth my own ideal
would be consummately revealed by him, then his
sombre eyes sparkled like the star of love ; there
was one hardly perceptible sob, and from that
time no other word ever passed between us on
the subject of this Third Act.'

" The days of these representations and the
dress rehearsal before the King were, without
doubt, for Wagner the culminating point in his
destiny as composer : they included those in-
effable hours that repay for a whole lifetime of
efforts, of disappointments, of miseries—his ' ideal
realised,' the splendour of his genius shining
before his own eyes and penetrating his very
being with a glorious certainty.

" And what a magnificent trinity, Richard
Wagner, Ludwig II. and the incarnation of Tristan!
What a noble joy animated them all ! ' How
I bless those hours ! ' cried Schnorr, in a burst
of enthusiasm. ' O Master, with your help and

the help of this divine king, I also must accomplish
something great and glorious ! '

" A most unusual interruption brought this
splendid manifestation of art to an unforeseen
conclusion after the fourth representation. From
the first, Wagner had felt for Schnorr's prodigious
achievement an astonishment full of respect, which
increased to dread and finally became an actual
terror. It was unbelievable that the singer could
repeat this performance day after day, after the
custom of the theatre. The Master felt that it
would be a crime, and he therefore declared that
this fourth representation of *Tristan* should be
the last ; that he would not permit another.
So the work was not given again.

" ' I feel that I have no right to inflict such a
condition of trouble upon a human being,' said
Wagner.

" It was not a question of physical fatigue—
Schnorr did not experience any : but to live
Tristan, to burn with his passions, to suffer his
agonies, to thrill with his ecstasies, to die his
death !—such superhuman exaltation, such emotion and fever of the soul, all this the Master could
not permit again. So the success was interrupted,

the big receipts were cut off, for such secondary
considerations as these did not concern those
generous minds for an instant.

" Then a very great project began to take shape
in Wagner's brain.

" ' With the certainty of the unspeakable importance of Schnorr for my musical creations, a
new springtide of hope entered into my life. The
medium was at last found through which my
creative power could link itself to the present.
The moment was come in which to teach and to
make clear. That which had been universally
misunderstood, denounced as unplayable, mocked
at, covered with contempt, was about to be
proved an undeniable artistic reality. To create
a German style for representing works of German
genius—this was our watchword. And with this
consoling hope I found it easier to oppose, for the
time, any further productions of *Tristan*. This
work and these representations were so different
from the usual performances that they would
necessitate too sudden a leap into the unknown ;
the precipices and chasms yawning before it must
be approached deliberately. We must begin by
carefully roofing them over, by paving the way

toward ourselves, the isolated artists, up to our
summit, for those associates that were indispensable to us. So then, Schnorr being ours,
it was determined to found a Royal College of
Music and Dramatic Art.'

"Alas! how many obstacles, how many fresh
struggles, and before the work could be achieved,
how cruel the death that struck down the hero, in
the fulness of youth, in the fulness of beauty!"

And now, when in the gallery I pass before the
superb likeness of Schnorr von Karolsfeld, I in
my turn feel my heart contract, and I stifle a
cry of anger, of revolt, against so blind and imbecile
a destiny.

XXVIII

To-day it happened that when we entered the
drawing-room at Tribschen we found our host
there entertaining strangers, visitors! A gentle-
man and a lady, both very small in figure and
rather dull in aspect, were sitting with an air
of constraint, only one of them speaking.

The Master presented them.

"His Excellency The Counsellor Isérof and

Madame Isérof, who have come from Russia to see me."

We exchanged some rather cold salutations.

It was evident that our presence displeased the newcomers as much as theirs disturbed us. They felt that we were more intimate than they in the household; they saw that we were received very cordially, that Russ and Cos did not bark, but gave evidence of pleasure in our arrival. Yet these people were much older acquaintances of Wagner's than were we; they certainly would have preferred to have the Master to themselves. Ah! how well we could comprehend what they felt!

Madam Cosima followed me out on to the steps. We both leaned against the iron railing, and she told me about the visitors.

" Counsellor Isérof is a composer well thought of in Russia, who is worthy of being admitted into the free-masonry of the brotherhood if only to uphold firmly the Wagnerian standard at Petersburg. Of his wife there is not much to say. She seems to be rather in the background. They are going, as you are, to Munich, to be present at the production of the *Rheingold*."

"Well, between soldiers of the same army there must be good understanding."

"Indeed yes. The Master will undoubtedly keep them to supper."

"Very well. We must be very amiable to Isérofitus and Isérofita ! "

XXIX

As the weather was beautiful and very warm, Madam Cosima bathed in the lake nearly every day with her little girls, and I was invited to join in this cool recreation.

Under the shadow cast by the little shed of the landing-place, which deepened the blue of the limpid water, we very prudently disported ourselves. Madam Cosima and the children wore long white dressing-gowns ; she, with her blond hair hanging in braids, seemed like a saint surrounded by cherubs, or even a swan guiding her brood. I, myself, was in a bathing costume, and so I ventured beyond the prescribed limits into the clearer blue and the sunlight, cutting capers, and feeling very flattered by the admiration which my ease and audacity as a swimmer aroused among those who could not leave the shelter.

But, when I had gone a little too far away, and
a chorus of clear, sweet voices called me back
with cries and supplications, then I returned very
obediently and stood again in shallow water,
and joined with the merry circle in madly splashing
the water into the air, laughing with them as it
fell again in showers of pearls.

XXX

Alas ! we had only a few more days to remain
in Lucerne. The opening of the Exposition of
Painting was announced and we must be there,
in order to fulfil our engagements with the journals
to which we had promised our letters.

On one of these last days the weather was
dull and stormy, and Madam Cosima and I had
stayed under the great pine that the Master was
so agile in climbing.

He had gone to his room to work for a time
on his study of Beethoven. Madam Cosima
was giving me information about Munich, telling
me what was best to see there : among other
things the gallery of Count von Schack, an
original character even more interesting, per-

haps, than his collection, which contained, among many daubs, a few fine paintings.

" You will also see my father, and someone who is very dear to him," added she.

As she spoke these words an expression of sadness passed quickly over her face and as quickly disappeared.

" I feel sure," she continued, " that you have no idea for whom your father wrote the ' *Symphonie en blanc majeur.*' You do not know ' *La femme Cygne,*' ' *La neige Vierge,*' ' *L'Hostie,*' ' *La moelle de Roseau,*' or who was the original of those delightful portraitures."

" Then there was an original ? "

" Yes, madame ; before you were born that original inspired the poet who was your father, and at that time, it appears, his description was very like her."

" Do you know who she was ? "

" The very person about whom I spoke a moment ago, and who, I am certain, will be curious to see you. She was born a Nesselrode, then became Madam Kalergic, and is to-day the Countess Muchanoff. Very enthusiastic about Wagner, she has been for a long time devoted to his cause.

Intelligent, cultured, a musician! My father
asserts that no one interprets Chopin as well
as she does."

" Then there is a connection between you ? "

" Yes."

" What bitterness in that ' Yes ! ' What has
she done to you ? "

" I believed that I could count upon her friendship, and she failed me at the moment when I
had most need of it. Last winter she overwhelmed me with reproaches because I did not
take her into my confidence regarding the distrac-
tions of my inner life. I replied quietly that I
had nothing to confide, nothing to conceal. ' The
painful situation in which I am placed will dis-
entangle itself very naturally, since Herr von
Bülow and I are agreed upon the divorce.' But
my father, with whom I am no longer in touch,
struck the last blow at me, in dissuading Herr
von Bülow from this project. I wrote at once to
Madam Muchanoff, begging her to use her influence with my father. I besought her to prevent
him from influencing Herr von Bülow in a way
so contrary to my interest and my dearest wishes.
She has done nothing. Her reply was confused,

without sympathy and without frankness. Ah! how I regret having broken through my reserve with her, and, above all, having allowed Wagner to write to her as he has done, so open-heartedly and with so much enthusiasm! But, hush! here he comes again. I do not want him to see that I am sad."

XXXI

Behind the house, in that court which formed a part of the garden, and from which the carriage-drive started, there was a high swing, which the children were allowed to use very carefully, and with which the older people sometimes amused themselves. One day Madam Cosima was sitting on the narrow board. Wagner offered to start the swing and give her a good flight through the air.

All went well for a time, but, little by little, the motion became more rapid; higher and still higher went the swing! In vain Madam Cosima begged for mercy. Carried away by a kind of frenzy, the Master paid no attention, and the incident began to have a terrifying aspect.

Cosima grew white; her hold relaxed, and she was about to fall.

" Do you not see that she is fainting ? " I cried, throwing myself toward Wagner.

He grew pale, in his turn, and the danger was quickly averted. But, as the poor woman continued to be dizzy and trembling, the Master concluded it would be wise to create a diversion. He ran rapidly toward the house, and by the aid of the shutters, the mouldings and projections of the stones, he climbed nimbly up the side, and reaching the balcony of the floor above, leaped over it.

He had obtained the desired effect, but in replacing one evil by another. Trembling with anxiety, Cosima turned to me, saying under her breath :

" Above all things, do not notice him ; do not look surprised, or you can never tell where he will end."

XXXII

" While you are in Munich," Wagner said to me, " try to induce them to show you the model of a theatre that the great architect Semper constructed for me. I warn you that this will not be easy, even with the introductions that I shall

G

be able to give you. They have consigned this
model to some out-of-the-way corner of the palace,
and they are not fond of bringing it to light.
They strongly suspect that I have not altogether
given up the hope that one day I may see my
buried project come to life again, and this pre-
sentiment is a real nightmare for my enemies."

A little later Madam Cosima drew me to one
side, and said :—

"If you should be able, in connection with the
approaching representation of the *Rheingold*, to
bring before the public the history of that theatre
project, which the Master told you about, I do
not believe that I can be mistaken in saying that
you would give him a real and profound satisfaction ; for the truth about those events has
been so completely disfigured by envy, incapacity,
and spite as to be hardly recognisable."

"You may be very sure that I will gladly do
what I can."

"It is just because I am sure of your devotion to
this noble cause that I make my petition to you."

"But I know nothing about the project. Where
can I get the information necessary in order not
to be misleading ? "

" Of course I will tell you all about it, as briefly and clearly as I can. Come upstairs with me to my dressing-room; there you can take notes."

This *boudoir*, on the first floor, was a little room, with wall coverings and draperies of green silk, and situated in a corner of the house. It overlooked the garden and, through the trees, one could see the blue of the lake and the violet shadows of the mountains. I had already passed many hours in this room, Madam Cosima having had the kindness to read to me there the Hindoo history of Nal and Damayanti, translating it from the German. I was searching just then for biographies of illustrious lovers of all countries, having promised to contribute a series of portraitures for the publication contemplated by the Editor Lecroix, and entitled "Les Grandes Amoureuses." Jean Richepin, Zola, and others collaborated in this work, which, for some reason, was never completed. A few portraitures only appeared in print, but not in the order of succession, and the greater number of the manuscripts were scattered.

I installed myself in my accustomed place on

a little divan fitted into the corner. Madam
Cosima seated herself in front of me, her elbows
resting on the table. She was charming so,
in the full light, and with her crown of heavy
blond hair. Her soft blue eyes shone with a
tender light; a pleased smile half disclosed her
pretty teeth. We were both delighted at the idea
of planning something which might give pleasure
to the Master!

I took a pencil and paper, and listened with all
my ears.

" Perhaps you do not know," said she, " that
Wagner was condemned to death in Saxony,
for having taken part in the revolution of '49.
As he fled, in company with others, he owed
his escape to a singular chance. In a village
near the frontier, his companions were seized,
but they did not see Wagner, who was asleep
in an out-of-the-way corner of the hall of the
inn."

" Wagner condemned to death ! "

" It is incredible, is it not ? But you must
not imagine that he was a very fierce democrat.
He was occupied only with questions of art, and,
like Walther of the *Meistersinger*, he was chiefly

in revolt against the tyranny of routine. He sincerely believed that a political upheaval would lead to an artistic reform; he has paid for that error by twelve years of exile. Defeated as the insurrection was, he still clung to the illusion that better times would surely come for his country and for art. So then it was that, alone, cut off from the world, with nothing to live for, he conceived, in view of those better times, the plan of his tetralogy, of a great national drama, which should make to live before the regenerated German people the gods and heroes of ancient Germanic mythology. Years passed; the better times never came, and the life of the exile grew more and more bitter. Yet, beyond any doubt, Richard Wagner became a celebrated and popular composer throughout all Germany. Thanks to the intervention of my father, *Tannhäuser* and *Lohengrin* had been given in Weimar, and also in other capital cities. The exigencies of his life would not permit of his disdaining the situation which now offered itself. The Master was aware that he would have to come down from the heights of his dream and follow this more accessible path which opened before him. In 1857, therefore, he interrupted the composition of the Ring of the Nibelungen, of which the *Rheingold*, the *Valkyrie* and two acts of *Siegfried* were completed."

"What! was he already so far advanced in that tremendous work?"

"Yes. And then Wagner performed another miracle : he composed *Tristan and Isolde*! When the amnesty was finally granted to him, he went back to Germany. He saw what was happening there with regard to matters of art, and that he could not dream of producing his tetralogy. However, he published the poems from it, preceded by a preface wherein he pointed out in a supremely able way the steps that ought to be taken to attain to the creation of a great National Art. Then he applied himself to the composition of his *Meistersinger*. When the King of Bavaria summoned Wagner, he had read this preface, and the first thing he said to him was, ' Finish your Nibelungen. I feel that I am called to help you realise your vision.'

"And so it was decided to build a theatre that should be absolutely independent of daily representations and of change of programme. A theatre the opening of which, occurring only

once a year, should be an artistic consecration.
But what architect would be capable of constructing this monument according to the ideas of the
Master? None other than Semper, the designer
of the Dresden Museum and theatre, an artist of
the first rank, whose talents were unquestioned.
The King gave him the command to draw up the
plans. Just at this time a formidable intrigue
was organised, which revealed itself in a succession
of spiteful acts, outrages, and furious onslaughts
against him whose only dream was to endow
his country with a superior art. This reached
such a point that Wagner, fearing for his royal
friend, withdrew from Munich. But Ludwig II.
would not let go his prize. He banished the
principal promoters of these villainies, among
others the Minister Pforten, to a distance; and
the negotiations with Semper on the subject of
the theatre were continued.

" The enemies were conquered only in appearance. They broke loose again and, after an
exhausting struggle, too long to recount, it was
found necessary to give up the building of
the theatre. Once more Wagner retired. He
came to Tribschen, and again took up his

interrupted work, after an interval of ten
years.

"The King only asks of him the completion
of this tetralogy, and it is his wish to produce
the different parts of it, from year to year, in his
own theatre, since the foolishness and malignity
of those about him will not allow of the carrying
out of Semper's plans. But Wagner has sworn
that he will not be present at any of these fragmentary representations of his work. He con-
siders himself as virtually exiled from Bavaria.
So, for the second time, Destiny has reserved for
him the trial of not being present at the performances of his own works, and of not hearing
the resounding music of his immense orchestra.
That is the fate imposed upon him to-day, by
his artistic conscience.

"There, dear friend, is the history of the defeat
of a man of genius by a horde of envious imbeciles.
I am sure that Wagner will be glad if you re-
establish the truth about this affair which has
been so abominably misrepresented.

"And now let us hurry down. They have
probably already noticed our absence."

MADAME COSIMA WAGNER.

XXXIII

Villiers had promised Wagner to read him his one-act play *La Révolte,* which the younger Dumas, who admired it very much, had caused to be accepted at " The Vaudeville," the plan being to produce it the following winter. Villiers had always postponed this serious reading. But finally on the evening before the last day of our stay, as we were saying good-night, they called out to him not to forget to bring the manuscript when we should return on the morrow.

Villiers was ambitious to be a great actor— perhaps he was one ; for a long time his mind was possessed by a single idea, that of learning the *rôle* of Hamlet and interpreting it better than anyone else had ever done. He had even expended very considerable sums on the preparation of a suitable costume, of black velvet and jet, which he often put on and, standing before a mirror, passed whole nights in trying different effects. At this time a pair of padded tights was all that remained of the costume, and Villiers sometimes wore them on social occasions, when he wished to have beautiful legs.

The reading of *La Revolte*, at Tribschen, was a glorious moment for the author of that work.

When he read or declaimed, there was no longer any question of inarticulate speech or broken phrasing. He enunciated the text in a clear and resonant voice, and with such perfect art that both the characters and the sentiments were wonderfully distinct.

He was listened to in a religious silence, with extreme attention and an increasing interest.

It is certain that if the play fell, in "The Vaudeville," before the Philistines whom it scourged, it was avenged in advance on this evening, when it went off with shining success.

"You are a true poet," said Wagner to the author, who was greatly elated, "and I should like to see you turn upon the ideal world, more important than the real for artists like us, the same searching gaze with which you have penetrated the material world. I should like to see you draw forth from there types as living as those which you have just evoked."

Villiers explained, very clearly this time, that it was in defence of the ideal that he had created this character—a woman haunted by lofty aspirations, yet married to a man who was of the earth earthy, utterly incapable of understanding her, and constantly torturing her without knowing it.

" A feminine Prometheus," concluded he, " whose vitals are devoured by a goose ! "

The evening was prolonged as much as possible, but the time came, all the same, for the farewells and separation. It was agreed upon that we should pass a few more days here on our return from Munich, as the shortest route back to Paris is certainly by way of Tribschen.

A last time, then, we drove in Wagner's carriage along the dark roads, and after it had left us at the hotel, we listened for a long time to the sound of the wheels and the beating of the horses' hoofs, becoming gradually fainter and fading away, little by little, into the night. . . .

Early next morning, when we came out of the Hôtel du Lac to go to the station, whom should we find waiting for us, but Russ, the beautiful Newfoundland !

He sometimes came alone to see us in this way, but on this especial day and at such an hour it was truly very singular ! Was it because he had an intimation of some change, or had they sent him to bear us a last salute?

Very gratified and very much touched, we responded to his caresses, and it was upon his great, kind head that, with sincere emotion, we pressed the kiss of farewell.

PART SECOND

I

A HEAVY sky, a foggy atmosphere and the warm rain that falls without a sound : the weather is entirely in unison with our sentiments ! No more blue sky, no more sun : all is gray around us as within us. The lake of Constance, upon which we sail to reach Bavaria, appears quite ugly under the mist, after the lake of Lucerne which was for us so blue and limpid ! Yet this water which bears us, and which, alas ! is not the same that bathes the dear promontory with its tall poplars, bears us nevertheless toward a pre-destined country, toward the Theatre-Temple where the rites of our religion are fulfilled.

But this melancholy must be driven away, and it is Villiers who makes the charge. Still full of pride over his success of the evening before, he is unable to stop thinking and speaking of it.

" *Hein!* How he listened ! What a public ! How pleased I was ! "

And again his laugh rings out : his spirit kindles
through the obscurities of his speech.

During breakfast we install ourselves upon the
deck under the shelter of a dripping canvas.
And what a breakfast !   An omelet harder
than a pancake, and filled with a stuffing the
nature of which defies all speculation.

" Yellow turnips ! " hazards Villiers.

" It can't be yellow turnips. It is more like
bits of raw pumpkin."

We consult the *Speisekarte* and find " Omelet
with Apricots."   Quarters of unripe apricot in
an overcooked omelet—what an infernal com-
bination ! O Shade of Brillat-Savarin ! [1] Our
delicate French epicurism is doubtless about to
be put to a rude test by the barbarously heavy
German cooking.

But even so ! Is not the drinking horn of the
pilgrim still hanging from our shoulders ?   Does
not the staff still burden our hands ? Roots
torn from the earth, muddy water from the
brooks, even these things ought to content us.

True ! And surely one can see that it is only
in the sincerest charity, in order to give them a

[1] Author of "The Physiology of Taste."

pleasure, that we bestow upon the fishes of the lake that " Omelet with Apricots."

At Lindau the boat stops and we enter Bavaria. And here we are stirred by a new emotion at the thought of treading this soil, of being in the land of Ludwig II., the young king of the Graal, whom we ourselves have also chosen for our King. Here all speaks of him, all things bear his colours and his crest : the time-tables, the gates, the letter-boxes are painted in white and blue : the royal crown in chiselled bronze is everywhere to be seen, surmounting the coat of arms with its lozenge of blue and silver, which upholds the lions rampant ; " *Königreich Bayern,*" [1] these words are on all sides, on the façades, on the arch of the station, on the railway carriages.

During the journey to Munich we try to recall everything that Wagner has told us about the king : best of all is Wagner's first interview with the messenger whom the king had sent, and who, after searching vainly for a long time, finally discovered the unfindable great man.

This was at Stuttgart : Wagner had stopped there after fleeing from Vienna. During many

[1] Kingdom of Bavaria.

months, in the Opera-house of that city, he had
directed the rehearsals of "*Tristan and Isolde.*"
His hotel-keeper—having long since presented his
bill, was kept patient by expectations of the
fruitful receipts of the first night.

But after seventy rehearsals, and a very few
representations, by reason of disaffection and
intrigue the work was declared impossible and the
company broke up. The danger of detention for
debt still existed; Wagner dreaded this above
all things, he had not sufficient resources with
which to satisfy his creditors, but falling back
upon a project for a series of concerts in
Russia, he had left Vienna. That plan also fell
through.

Discouragement and bitter despair again over-
came him, and he believed that from that hour
he should no longer have the force to retrieve
himself. In the most sombre humour, he was
making his preparations to leave Stuttgart when
an attendant of the hotel where he was staying
brought to him a visiting card upon which he
read : " Von Pfistermeister, Aulic Secretary to
His Majesty the King of Bavaria."

How could he foresee that this little slip of

paper marked the end of all his troubles, and that happiness was in store for him ?

Wagner suspected that it might be some creditor in disguise, and refused to receive the unknown person. But the visitor insisted, saying that King Ludwig had sent him and that he could not be denied.

When the announcer of miracles appeared he at once put in the Master's hand the King's portrait, and a diamond ring. Ludwig II. wished to declare himself a most fervent admirer of the genius of Wagner, and offered to use all his power to aid him to finish his work and to realize his dreams. The messenger had received orders not to return without Richard Wagner.

Stirred by deep emotion, his face streaming with tears that he could not check, Wagner comprehended that misfortune was finally overcome, and that a treaty of sublime alliance was about to be made between himself and the royal disciple so suddenly revealed to him.

The first act of this eighteen-year-old king, who had ascended the throne less than a month before, was to render homage to an artist of genius, and to reach out to him a fraternal hand.

H

While Ludwig II., in his palace at Munich, awaited the arrival of Wagner with joyful impatience, a courtier wishing to flatter the sovereign, said to him :

" Men of genius equal to that of Wagner revisit the earth only once in a thousand years."

" A man with genius equal to that of Wagner," responded the king, " has never before come to this world, and he will never come again."

And Ludwig II., to the great scandal of his Court, ran hastily down the staircase of honour, to greet Richard Wagner.

That meeting was perhaps one of the most touching and memorable incidents of history.

Wagner retains a magical impression of it.

" The king is so comely, his thoughts are so elevated and his soul so noble," said he, " that I am afraid his life may pass athwart this vulgar world like a dream of the Gods.

" He knows and understands me like my own soul. He longs to remove all my troubles and embarrassments, and help me to accomplish my work ! "

We now know that in spite of his power and

his good will, the king was not able to attain
to the realization of all his desires.

The Archangel could not subdue the dragon,
so covered by the impenetrable breastplate formed
of human imbecility.

The sword dulled itself against that thick shell,
the crown narrowly escaped being shattered
thereon : the hatred and fury of the Philistines
against an artist of genius increased this time
to the point of riot. They howled in the streets,
they broke the windows of the Master's house,
until at last, fearing some misfortune for the royal
friend who persisted in defending him, he feigned
to separate himself from him, and quitted Munich.

If the king as chief of the State was unhappily
forced to give way before the popular tempest,
as friend he did not concede a single point, and
remained true to his faith.

In that dear retreat of Tribschen which Wagner
then found, forever delivered, thanks to the
royal friend, from the sordid troubles which
bedim the spirit, he had no longer any but
lofty cares, and, in retirement and peace, he
finished the " *Meistersinger* " and recommenced
work on the " Ring of the Nibelung."

II

The train puffed and panted as it laboured
up the slope which rises without interruption
from Lindau to Munich. We were already very
high up, for occasional mists of cloud drifted
across our carriage. Wonderful landscapes opened
before us ; far away peaks tearing the mist into
ribbons, glimpses of deep valleys soon lost to
sight, forests of pines, hills of a fresh velvety
green which undulated to the sky, and at the
stations of the infrequent hamlets and villages
which we passed, the blue and white of the royal
escutcheons always reappeared upon the gates
and arches.

" *Königreich Bayern* ! "   How happy we were
to be in the domain of King Charming ! We
thought and spoke only of him.

This same route, by which we were coming,
he once travelled in the opposite direction, alone
and in secret, in order to go and surprise the
Master at Tribschen and, " to experience again
during a few wonderful hours the joy of being
with him."

Wagner had told us the story of this journey of the King.

"It was the 22nd of May, 1866, on the fifty-third anniversary of my birth. Early in the morning the king had started out alone from the castle of Starnberg, riding his horse to Biesenhofen where he had taken the train to Lindau; there he disembarked, and to my profound astonishment, arrived that same afternoon at Tribschen. They set up a camp-bed for him in my study. He begged me to return with him to Bavaria, but, for his own sake, I felt that I must refuse.

In the following year, Ludwig II. was affianced to his cousin, the Archduchess Sophie, sister to the Empress of Austria, and, in order to add to the significance of the marriage ceremonies, fixed for the 12th October, they reserved for this date the first representation of "*Die Meistersinger.*" But, before that time arrived, one evening when "*Tristan*" was being given at the Royal Theatre, the prospective bride appeared in a box in an unceremonious toilet; she listened to the work with an absent air, and without attempting to disguise the fact that she was bored. She was not Wagnerian in her tastes! The discovery abruptly broke the spell : the King judged that a person who shared so little in his faith and his enthusiasm ought not to be his wife, and he closed his heart against her.

We admired him for that, and Villiers declared that if he understood German better he would compose a poem in which he would say magnificent things, and would send it to Ludwig II.

This idea led us back to the dedication printed at the beginning of the score of " *Die Walküre*," those well-known stanzas that Wagner addressed " To the royal friend," consecrating him in this way to an ever glorious immortality.

The verses are reputed to be untranslatable into French, and that fact naturally incited us to make the attempt. One of our number was thoroughly conversant with the language of Goethe, and for some time back we had been working at the translation. What a good chance to go on with it, during these hours of the journey !

In the original, Wagner's poem is very beautiful, with an unusual grace and exquisite subtlety of expression.

What would it be in French ?

Here is our attempt at a translation :

AU ROYAL AMI.

" O roi, doux seigneur qui protèges ma vie !
Toi qui revèles la suprême bonté,
Combien, arrivé au but de mes efforts, je m'efforce
De trouver le mot juste qui t'exprimerait ma gratitude !
Pour le dire ou l'écrire, comme je la cherche en vain !
Et pourtant, de plus en plus impérieux, m'entraîne le désir
De trouver ce mot qui exprimerait
Le sentiment de reconnaissance que je porte dans mon coeur.

Ce que tu es pour moi, je ne puis, émerveillé, m'en rendre compte
Qu'en évoquant ce que je fus sans toi . . .
Pas une étoile ne se leva pour moi, que je ne la visse pâlir ;
Pas un espoir que je n'eusse perdu.
Livré au bon plaisir, à la faveur du monde,
Aux jeux du gain et du risque,
Tout ce qui en moi luttait pour l'émancipation de l'art
Se vit trahi par le sort, sombra dans la bassesse.

Celui qui, jadis, commanda à la branche desséchée
De reverdir dans la main du prêtre,
Bien qu'il m'eût ravi tout espoir de salut
Et que la dernière illusion consolante se fût évanouie,
Fortifia en mon sein cette foi
En moi que je puisais en moi-même ;
Comme je lui demeurais fidèle,
Il fit refleurir pour moi la branche desséchée.

Ce que solitaire et muet je gardais au fond de moi
Vivait aussi dans le sein d'un autre ;
Ce qui agitait profondément et douloureusement l'esprit d'un homme
Emplissait d'un joie sacrée un coeur d'adolescent ;

Ce qui nous entraînait dans une ardeur printanière
Vers un même but,—conscient . . . inconscient . . .
Devait s'épancher comme une joie du printemps :
Double foi, faisant naître une frondaison nouvelle.

Tu es le doux printemps qui m'as paré à nouveau,
Qui as rajeuni la sève de mes branches et de mes ramures ;
C'est ton appel qui m'a fait sortit de la nuit,
De la nuit hivernale qui tenait inerte ma force ;
Ton altier salut, qui m'a charmé,
M'arrache à la souffrance dans une joie soudaine
Et je marche, à présent, fier et heureux, par de nouveaux
   sentiers,
Dans le royaume estival de la grâce. . . .

Quel mot pourrait donc te faire comprendre
Tout ce que tu es pour moi ?
Si je peux à peine exprimer le peu que je suis,
Toi, au contraire, tu es roi en tout.
Aussi la lignée de mes oeuvres repose-t-elle en toi,
Dans une paix bien heureuse.
Et puisque tu as comblé tous mes espoirs,
Délicieusement j'ai renoncê à l'espoir.

Donc je suis pauvre, je ne garde qu'une chose,
La foi à laquelle s'unit la tienne :
C'est elle, la puissance qui fait que je me montre fier,
C'est elle qui saintement trempe mon amour.
Mais si, partagée, cette foi est encore à moitié mienne
Elle sérait tout entière perdu pour moi si elle venait à te
   manquer :
Ainsi, c'est toi seul qui me donnes la force de te remercier
Grâce à ta foi royale et sans défaillance."

We had great difficulty in making this translation and were far from satisfied with it. But
there was no more time, the train was already

slowing up to the station, we had reached Munich
—*München* !

Outside the station, the omnibus which we took
for the hotel of " *Trois Rois Mages*," after going
a short distance was obliged to stop before
a military orchestra.   Fine looking, fair-haired
soldiers in sky-blue uniforms, were grouped about
their leader, and were playing nothing else than
the religious march from " *Lohengrin* ! "

Later on, Wagner, in fun, tried to make us
believe that we owed it to him that we had been
" so religiously received."

III

What an amusing city is Munich, with its
architectural follies ! I do not know another
outside of France which seems to me so attractive.
Ludwig I. probably had a great love for memorials,
and certainly, he hesitated at nothing. It was
he who wished to reproduce and bring together
in his capital, all the edifices which he had admired
in the course of his travels ; so this pretty city
resembles the " Rue des Nations " of some universal
exposition.

Do you love the Florentine style ? Here is

the library and its majestic marble staircase
leading to the " loggia dei Lanzi," copied exactly
from that of Florence ; a little farther on, under
the name of Königbau you will see a reproduc-
tion of the famous Pitti Palace. If you prefer
Roman art, the arch of Constantine is close at
hand, and you will also come across a fifteenth-
century dome. If it is Greek art that attracts
you, you may see the Propylæum of Athens,
the Glyptothek in the Ionic style, or the palace
of Fine Arts in the Corinthian style : or better
still, near a consecrated wood, the Hall of Fame.
If you dream of Venice, you have only to
listen to the fluttering wings of the pigeons of
Saint Mark's, who have, evidently, all migrated
to Munich !

There are some buildings like cathedrals, high
and loaded down with sculptures, but they are
of moulded terra-cotta. The Renaissance style
is well represented, the rococo abounds, Egyptian
art, even, is not forgotten. In order to com-
memorate a noble feat of arms, they have erected
a metal obelisk, modelled upon the monolith
of Luxor, but this one has not the merit of being
a single casting of bronze.

The International Exposition of Painting, ostensible reason for our journey, was, I think, very remarkable; it did honour to the group of artists who organized it and brought into prominence the Bavarian school of painting. But I am forced to admit that in spite of the very conscientious accounts that I published in I cannot remember how many journals, I recall only very confused memories of them. But I do remember one painter, perhaps forgotten to-day, who was then at the beginning of his career and was much talked of: Gabriel Max—I can still see in my mind his lovely martyr, who, in the whiteness of death seemed to sleep so easily upon the cross.

On the other hand, a visit to the Pinakothek made an ineffaceable impression upon me. The Rubens collection above all seemed to me superb: the artist triumphs there in all his fleshly glory— he is jubilant, dazzling!

And what perfect taste was shown in the placing of the canvases! What a sensible arrangement! As far as possible, each room held the works of a single master grouped upon a favourable back-ground and under a well managed lighting. In this way the intensity of effect was doubled. One experienced to the full the painter's charm, and the contrast between one master and another was startling. For instance in the hall of Van Dyck, as one entered after viewing the resplendent walls of the hall of Rubens, the subdued colouring gave the impression of restful and mysterious shadows, out of which seemed to steal wonderful white masks of a distinction that is without equal. Then, too, the catalogue, translated into French, did not lack amusement for us: one read such things as these:

" The Virgin is seated at evening before an edifice : at her knee the little Jesus seizes with the right hand the lung border of her robe."

" Vanity under the guise of a beautiful woman of luxurious form, supporting herself with the left hand which holds a dying candle, upon a round mirror."

" A wolf devours a lamb while a fox also enters there."

" A woman seated beside an ass which brays on the ground nursing her infant."

" Two dogs quarrel with a calf's head."

" Portrait of the Elector Maximilian fully braced."

" St Martin on white horseback."

" The Christ, after having suffered death, receives graciously the four repentant sinners."

It is a good thing to laugh a little !

IV

Each morning bills were posted, giving the
programmes of the music to be played in the
different beer-gardens of Munich during the two
o'clock dinner-hour. Numerous selections from
the Wagner operas appeared in these programmes,
and so we decided to leave the hotel of the " *Trois
Rois Mages* " and its commonplace table d'hôte
in order to take furnished apartments and be free
to choose the place for our meals according to
the musical menu. Behold us then, our resolution taken, rushing from one end of the city to
the other in search of the appointed restaurant,
and, once there, hobnobbing with its population,
whether turbulent students, or middle - class
families who love to dine to the sound of fiddles.

To us, who were so unaccustomed to them,
these restaurant orchestras seemed excellent, and
we had great pleasure in listening to the fragments
which we so rarely had the opportunity to hear

at home.   We were delighted to notice that the
dining public always gave an especially warm
reception to the selections from Wagner.

One day we went to a very distant restaurant
where the overture of " *Die Meistersinger* " was
to be played.   The orchestra was disposed in
a most extraordinary fashion.   In default of a
better place they had installed it upon the outside gallery of a châlet which was in the midst
of the garden, a narrow balcony where two
musicians could with difficulty sit abreast, so
that the whole number of the players extended
from one end to the other of the façade and the
double-basses were a long distance from the brass
instruments.   We left the table where we had
dined to find seats in the enclosure so that the
sounds should be less scattered, and took our
places in front of the balcony facing the leader,
who occupied the very centre.

Not far from us were seated three young men
who had also drawn near to the musicians, and who
scrutinised us secretly and persistently.   One of
them. a very fair blond, tall and slight, seemed to
me the perfect type of the German student ; he
had long hair, straight as a poker, of a colour

lighter than his face, and his delicate profile
recalled the portraits of Schiller.   One of his companions, whose golden beard and gold-rimmed eye-
glasses glistened in the sun, had an expressive face
which fairly radiated happiness and enthusiasm.
The third was rather small, and one could
hardly see his features through the disordered
profusion of his brown hair, his eyebrows and
his beard.   A white dog stayed close by his
side.

Suddenly I heard the young man with the golden
beard say, in a very audible voice, as he looked
at us.

" I'll wager it is they."

After the last notes of the overture of " *Die
Meistersinger*," as we applauded with all our might,
the group of strangers came nearer.

" No longer any doubt," one of them said,
" since they applauded."

And the young man with the golden beard
advanced without hesitation.

" I am Hans Richter—" said he as he saluted
us—" and you certainly must be the friends who
have just been visiting Richard Wagner.   The
Master wrote me to put myself at your service

and to act as your guide about Munich, but he did not tell me where to find you."

Hans Richter, the chief of Orchestra of the Royal Theatre, who would have the honour of conducting the " *Rheingold* ! "

After cordial greetings Richter presented his friends, first the heavily bearded man, then the other.

" Herr Scheffer, a Wagnerian fanatic. Herr Franz Servais, son of the celebrated Belgian violinist ; he has just come from Brussels to hear the " *Rheingold.*"

So the man who had appeared to be the personification of a German student was a Belgian composer !

All seated at the same table with foaming bocks before us, we quickly became acquainted, and found each other very congenial, since we served under the same banner. It appeared that they had been searching for us all over Munich. Our passage to the hotel of the Three Kings had been traced, but we had gone from there without leaving any address, and from that point they could find no clue. Herr Scheffer had been very keen to find us before this especial

CORNER OF JUDITH GAUTIER'S SALON.

day was over, and had applied to the police, but chance had forestalled them.

" We had promised," said Richter, " to conduct you to a reunion this evening, at the house of the Countess of Schleinitz. We shall all be there."

" Liszt will be there," exclaimed Servais, " he arrived in Munich yesterday, and you will also see the Countess Muchanoff."

" Liszt ! "

I thought of Cosima, and her sorrow at being disapproved of by her father : I felt I would rather not see him. But my companions had already joyfully accepted, and had arranged a meeting place for the evening, at eight o'clock.

V

The Countess of Schleinitz, wife of the minister of the royal house of Prussia, at whose house we met, was an extremely gracious little person, very small and delicate, even fragile. She spoke French like a Parisian, a French sparkling with wit and drollery, and in her glance there was a gleam of passion. One could have said :—

" Le Caprice a taillé son petit nez charmant . . ."

I

A little snub nose tip-tilted with an elegant impertinence. The charm of her smile was trebled by the dimples it made in her cheeks.

They did not fail to introduce me to a great number of people, whose names, few of them easy to remember, have escaped me. I recall that of Lenbach, the already illustrious painter, and I remember the beautiful head of Edward Schuré, with its inspired and slightly " absent " air.

The appearance of Franz Liszt astonished me.

I was evidently out of the running, I was ignorant of everything: why that long black cassock ? Was he a priest ? With that smooth-shaven face, had he also a tonsure in the locks that fell long and straight to his shoulders ? But what eyes, like a lion, what burning glances under the shaggy eyebrows ! What overmastering irony in the curves of the large mouth with its thin lips ! In the whole attitude what majesty, tempered with benevolence.

The entrance of Liszt caused an extreme excitement in the assemblage, and I became more and more surprised. Could it be that he was a saint ?

They showed such an extraordinary veneration for him, especially the women. They hurried toward him, and almost kneeling, kissed his hands, raising looks of ecstasy to his face.

But my attention was suddenly drawn to a woman who had arrived at the same moment—surely this must be she, the mysterious beauty who came from the north, in a whirlwind of snow, and herself whiter than the snow. The lady with eyes like Parma violets, whom the poets have sung with such longing, the Countess of Kalergis, now Countess Muchanoff. *La Symphonie en blanc majeur* herself in fact! As yet she was standing with her back to me, at the other side of the grand piano. People were crowding about her as she took their outstretched hands. She was tall, a muslin scarf covered her shoulders, her pale blond hair curled at the nape of her neck. I repeated under my breath some words from the well-known poem which she had inspired my father to write, so long ago :—

> " Conviant la vue enivrée
> De sa boréale fraîcheur
> A des régals de chair nacrée,
> A des débauches de blancheur.

Son sein, neige moulée en globe,
Contre les camélias blancs
Et le blanc satin de sa robe
Soutient des combats insolents.

Dans ces grandes batailles blanches,
Satins et fleurs ont le dessous,
Et, sans demander leurs revanches,
Jaunissent comme des jaloux.

.   .   .   .   .

De quel mica de neige vierge,
De quelle moelle de roseau,
De quelle hostie et de quel cierge
A-t-on fait le blanc de sa peau ? . . ."

Alfred de Musset was also a fervent admirer of this white idol, and later, Heinrich Heine paraphrased, in honour of her whom he called, "The Cathedral of the God Love," the verses of Theophile Gautier :

" Auprès d'elle la neige de l'Himalaya
    Paraît grise comme la cendre ;
    Le lis que sa main saisit, aussitôt, par le contraste
    Ou par jalousie, devient couleur de rouille . . ."

I really dreaded the moment when she would turn, and, as she made a movement to do so, I closed my eyes, to keep for a little longer the illusion of the past.

Almost at once I hear the rustling of silk close beside me ; a clear musical voice addresses me, sweetly modulated, with a slight Russian accent. The Countess Muchanoff seats herself beside me and presses my hand, as she assures me that there is no need for an introduction, for she has recognised me without hearing my name, and that having the same admirations, the same ardent beliefs, we must belong to the same ideal family and should love even before we know each other.

She seems a very great lady, very sure of herself, intelligent, and filled with a passionate love of art. I look for the white camellias near the snow of her breast—very marble-like, in truth, but with the help, perhaps, of pearl white and a touch of rice powder. Her face is regular, pale under the fair hair so cleverly arranged. Although they believe her to be too superior to linger over any artifices of coquetry, she undoubtedly seeks to retain and to prolong a beauty so celebrated, but she depends still more upon the graces of her mind, which time does not affect, upon her intellectual culture and her musical talent.

With a coaxing familiarity she makes a strong effort to win me, to inspire me with confidence, but I am haunted by the idea that she is prejudiced

against Cosima, that she has betrayed her friendship, and I find it an effort to respond to her
friendly advances, or to abandon my reserve.

Liszt in his turn approaches me ; he speaks of
my father, whom he knew; he has seen me as a
child and remembers me, although I have no
memory of him. I find that he has the very
suave manners of a priest—but how can he be
a priest, and why are all these women so taken
with him ? Just now they are greatly perturbed
at seeing him occupied with one who has made
no advances, and so they cluster about him
again, begging him to play something, teasing
him to sit down at the piano. This he refuses to
do and repulses them rather rudely, declaring
that it is Madame Muchanoff who ought to play,
that he himself has too much pleasure in listening
to her to seat himself at the piano when she is
present.

The Countess rises, nonchalant and disdainful,
she draws off her gloves slowly, and her smile
says plainly enough that she devotes herself only
to spare Liszt a drudgery, and that she is amused,
to the point of derision, at the jealous rage of all
those who will be forced to applaud her.

"L'ivoire, où ses mains ont des ailes,
Et, comme des papillons blancs,
Sur la pointe des notes frêles
Suspendent leurs baisers tremblants . . . "

These lines mingle, in my mind, with the phrases of the nocturne that the Countess plays. She is certainly talented ; but it seems to me that her playing lacks restraint, that she exaggerates and plays with too much abandonment.

After she had stopped playing Liszt offered me his arm to conduct me to the refreshment table, in the face of the envious and uncomprehending glances of the greater number of the women. He allowed every one else to pass before us, with the idea, no doubt, of withdrawing with me a little to one side. In fact, as soon as we were alone, he said to me in a low voice :—

" You have seen Cosima ? "

I had none of that sentiment which the high personality of Liszt evoked among his intimates. I was absolutely ignorant of the beauty of his compositions, which I was to admire so much in the future, and of the incomparable loftiness of his character. I considered him only as a very

celebrated pianist. So I was not in the least
intimidated, and, believing him to be hostile to
the best interests of his daughter, it was with a
decided vehemence that I replied to him :—

" I beg of you, do not say anything against
your daughter to me. I am her partisan to such
an extent that I cannot admit any blame. In
the face of a personality so superhuman as Richard
Wagner's, the prejudices and even the laws of
men cannot prevail. Who would not feel the
fascination and submit joyfully to the supremacy
of such a genius ? In Cosima's place, you would
do as she does, and it is your duty as a father not
to put any obstacle in the way of the realization
of the great event to which she has the right to
look forward."

Liszt grasped me warmly by the arm.

" I am entirely of your opinion, but I may not
express it," said he in a still lower voice. " The
habit which I wear imposes certain opinions
which I cannot openly deny. I know the tempta-
tions of the heart too well to judge severely :
conventions force me to be silent, but within
myself, I desire more than anyone else for a legal
solution of this painful affair. I can do nothing

to hasten it ; as to retarding it in any way whatever, I have never had such a thought."

Greatly surprised and relieved I cried out,
impulsively—

" Will you authorise me to write that to
Cosima ? "

" Certainly," he replied. " I wished to ask you
to do so. Assure her that there is no need of a
rupture between us, that my heart is with her,
but that she ought to comprehend my reserve,
and to show, before the world, a certain consideration with respect to me, until the new order of
things is established."

" I will write this very evening. If you could
know what relief and what happiness this news
will give them."

" I am very glad of that. You see how I have
seized the first opportunity that has offered to
make known to my daughter, secretly, my inner-
most thought. I have sought for such an opportunity without finding it. In whom could I
confide ? Envy and hypocrisy find a place in
all human hearts. Very few have your frankness
and your beautiful, unrestrained enthusiasm. . . .
But let us go in. I believe that we are watched,

and that people are already surprised by our long conversation."

In fact many anxious and irritated looks were directed toward us, and, if the eyes of the women clustered there, had been daggers, I should never have passed the threshold of the dining-room alive.

During the refreshment hour Villiers de l'Isle-Adam talked with the Countess Muchanoff, who appeared to be struck with amazement. He had pinned upon his evening coat the decoration of the Knights of Malta, a little cross set with white enamel, and he explained to her that he was Grand Master of that order, which had been bestowed upon one of his ancestors in 1520. France not recognizing the knighthood of Malta, he could only wear the insignia when abroad. Then, at least, he could wear them conscientiously.

Villiers then proceeded to recount the complicated and confused history of his incontestable claims to the throne of Greece, by reason of this Grand-mastership. He had even, upon a time, presented his claim as a candidate for the royal succession, and had had a memorable campaign in the effort to maintain it.

From heraldic fantasies and aristocratic vanities, Villiers passed, happily, to the more reasonable pride of the poet : he narrated his reading at Wagner's house and his glorious success, and, when they separated, he had promised the Countess Muchanoff to give, at the *Hôtel des Quatre Saisons*, on any evening which she should be pleased to name, a second reading of *La Révolte*.

VI

We very soon became intimate with Franz Servais, and grew to regard him as our good friend. It was through him that I tried to penetrate some of the mysteries that seemed to me to envelope the life of Liszt, and first of all I asked how, and why, he was a priest ?

" It was only four years ago that he took the orders," said Servais to me, " and became the Abbé Liszt."

" In what way, and why ? "

" No one knows ! On his return from a journey to Rome, he was a priest. Perhaps he wished, in this way, to explain to the world, which had been in a state of excitement over his projects of marriage with the Princess Wittgenstein, that

they were definitely abandoned. I believe also
that he was relieved at being able to take away
from all the women who adored him, the hope of
obtaining his hand."

" But as a matter of fact, all the women seem,
even now, to quarrel over him quite openly. Does
not his habit make a difference to them ? "

" No, on the contrary, it inflames them the
more, it has all the fascination of forbidden
fruit ! Liszt exercises, moreover, an extraordinary influence over the women and even the men
who understand and admire him. I am able to
speak of this with knowledge, because I submit
to it myself without attempting to defend myself,
and I am proud to be one of his pupils. But
some of the women undoubtedly go too far. It
leads them into a sort of idolatry, of fetichism.
They dispute over a flower that he has touched,
they gather up the ends of his cigars, and those
who are sufficiently independent, and are able to
do so, follow him from city to city, all through
the year."

" And does not that exasperate him ? "

" On the contrary, he would be very unhappy
without the atmosphere of adoration which sur-

JUDITH GAUTIER IN BRITTANY.

rounds him. He loves the incense of these excessive flatteries. He feels the need of this mystical kingdom, and in order to hold it together, he distributes his favours, very simply, according to the merits of the recipients, or in the order of his own preferences."

" But how is he able to maintain order and harmony in his harem, and to keep down jealousy and rivalry ? "

" That is the most wonderful thing about it all," said Servais ; " he succeeds in keeping peace amongst all his votaries, he even makes them accept and respect a favourite. When you express astonishment at an abnegation so unusual among women, he makes to you this unexpected announcement, ' They love themselves in me.' "

VII

Wagner had telegraphed from Tribschen to the king, to tell him that some French friends, who had arrived in Munich, would be happy to see representations of *Lohengrin, Tannhäuser* etc., while they waited for the *Rheingold*. *Lohengrin* had already been announced. But, further than that, a servant in blue and gold livery brought us, each morning, admissions to the *galerie noble,* sometimes for the Royal Opera, sometimes for the Théâtre de la Résidence; it was by order of the king that we were accorded this favour, and we had the great pleasure, alas! for the French alone a rare one, of being present nearly every evening at productions of the tragedies and comedies of Shakespeare, alternating with operas of Wagner.

In its relation to the theatre, the love which the Bavarians feel for reconstruction and imitation produces the best of results : the plays are very carefully mounted, and the scenic effects very fine and exact. We had the pleasure of seeing, in the space of a few weeks, *Richard III., A Winter's Tale, As You Like It, Twelfth Night, Two Gentlemen of Verona, Lohengrin, The Flying Dutchman, Tannhäuser,* and *The Mastersingers.*

VIII

I was very glad to meet Liszt again at the soirée given for Villiers de l'Isle-Adam by the Countess Muchanoff. Very soon after my entrance

I recognized that he, also, was impatient to speak to me, for he threw me a questioning look, and as soon as we could draw a little away from the others he said to me :—

" Well, what news ? "

Then I told him how my letter, repeating his words, had caused a commotion of joy at Tribschen, had given them a blessed release from harrowing cares, and the consolation of knowing that the affection of a heart so dear was not lost. From that certainty they could draw strength for the struggle to come ! As for me, simply the messenger, the master had sent me his blessing.

Liszt, his eyes shining with tears quickly dried, seized my hand and rapidly whispered to me :

" Guard well the secret that I confide to you ; I will do my best on my return to Italy, to stop a few hours at Lucerne in order to embrace my daughter and my grandchildren."

And then he, who always refused to play, went to the piano, lifted the cover with a quick movement, and ran his masterful fingers over the keys in an impetuous, thrilling and passionate improvisation.

The ovation which this called forth approached delirium, but he hardly noticed it.

It was now the turn of Villiers to charm the audience. Well curled, his Maltese cross in the right place on his left side, he looked very magnificent. Yet he appeared to me a little nervous and disturbed. . . . Was it possible that the vast ornate drawing-room of the mansion overwhelmed him, and that this gathering of noble, well-dressed ladies, of high functionaries, of artists, forming a half circle as in a theatre, and staring at him in silent attention, abashed him more than the Olympian intimacy of Tribschen? In full light, standing at the end of the grand piano, he seemed to hesitate, he did not speak. But at last, with a proud toss of his head, he threw back his waving hair and began to read in a firm, clear voice.

I was reassured; Villiers, very certain of himself, was taking plenty of time and managing his effects; the audience was interested, a flattering murmur followed certain passages, they applauded; then again, the respectful silence was renewed, and they listened intently.

But, alas! What is happening? Suddenly Villiers is silent, he drops his manuscript and looks at his audience with wide open eyes filled with fright. With an hysterical gesture he unhooks the belt of his trousers, then he takes off his shoes and seats himself on the top of the piano. Oh, horror! What can he mean? Is that in the play? A mystification? A wager? In any case it is in very bad taste! There is a mocking uproar and everyone rises; they come to me; they question me.

What can I say? How can I make them understand that Villiers believes himself in danger of death, and that therefore he has done what he thinks is best for himself, irrespective of propriety. He has had, without doubt, a little nervous spasm of the heart; some physician, chaffing him, perhaps, once told him that if anything of the kind happened, he must loosen his clothing quickly, take off his shoes and stockings, and seat himself high up so that his feet would hang. And now they can see that the invalid has conformed to this order in every particular.

Much laughter was stifled behind fans. They pretended to forget the incident.

Villiers had fled, bearing his shoes with him, while our little group, not daring to follow him in beating a retreat, remained feeling very much

K

embarrassed, and experiencing the isolation of the vanquished.

Franz Servais was filled with consternation; he walked about feverishly, his hands in his pockets, the long pale wisps of his hair hanging and almost meeting again in his mouth, which constantly opened to give vent to vehement recriminations.

"There is only one thing that can save the situation," cried he. "There is only one excuse that Villiers can make. Death! Yes, yes, for the honour of us all he must die!"

IX

We had taken furnished apartments in Maximilianstrasse, a remarkably wide street, very gay and attractive with its rows of fine shops and fascinating shop-windows. It begins in the heart of Munich, close to the Royal Theatre, and, extending for over a mile, ends at the Isar, a very impetuous river, running madly over enormous stones, which appear to have been artifically cut. These stones, by their sharp angles, form giant steps over which the water dashes in cascades. We did not imagine this torrent to be navigable,

but one day an unexpected sight proved to us
that it was so.

On this very warm day, we slowly sauntered
toward the Isar, hoping to find a little freshness
in the gardens, which on the other side of the
river, extend the whole length of the wide banks.
Having stopped in the middle of the bridge, above
a dizzying tumult of waters, we suddenly beheld
in the distance four or five rafts loaded with men,
which seemed to be at the mercy of the current,
but were, on the contrary, very skilfully guided as
they swept along.

" Savages !   Pirogues ! " cried Villiers.

And in fact it was a spectacle that suggested
only adventurous savages shooting the rapids
in canoes made from the bark of trees.

The shallowness of the water as it ran over the
rocks added to the danger of being drowned that
of being crushed to pieces at the slightest error
in the difficult manœuvring. We had scarcely
time to tremble for these men, or even to distinguish them, standing on the rafts and leaning
on their short poles, before they had passed under
the bridge, and flying from the other side had
disappeared from sight.

" The true course to the Abyss ! " cried Villiers.

" Where do these beings come from ? " I demanded, " and whither do they go ? "

" Ah, it is better not to know. It is never good to investigate too deeply. We have seen a vision, have we not, of ferocious warriors descending the Ogowe, in the pursuit of a rival tribe : why should we try to convince ourselves that we have only seen worthy peasants going to the nearest market, for the very prosaic purpose of selling some vulgar product of the soil ? "

" In any case they are brave as well as worthy peasants ! "

But Villiers was no longer listening : his imagination had followed the warriors of the Ogowe and was wandering far away, and the part of the man that was left with us expressed itself in a confused monotone, mingled with laughter. He toyed with his ideas, as one amuses oneself at the seashore, by letting the sand fall in cascades between the fingers. But I well knew that there were some precious stones in the sand that Villiers sifted, and I lay in wait for these.

When we were finally seated on grassy hillocks

in the shadows of the great trees of the English Garden, where we could look out over the fresh meadows starred with saffron blossoms like thousands of goblin fires, and the nearer willows, of a vivid green, with long strands trailing in the Isar, then at last I began to distinguish some light amid the obscurities of the discourse of Villiers.

" I have a glimpse of a misty sea, a dreamlike twilight around an unknown isle, then, in a luminous eddy, a great sphinx emerges from the waves and swims toward the bank. Across her back a violet banner is floating, and on the banner in letters of gold gleams the word : Inviolata ! "

" And that is all," said Villiers; " it will never connect itself with anything and will never be explained. The intense impression, the charm, the mystery, the disquieting strangeness, are all in the picture itself, seen through an opening in the clouds, and never more to be forgotten."

" And there are some poems," added he, " which should have but a single stanza : this one for example :—

' La lourde clé du rêve à ma ceinture sonne . . .' [1]

---

[1] Forever clanks at my girdle the heavy key of the dream.

Isn't that complete enough? Isn't that magnificent? What could one add to that? In my foolishness and desire to make a poem I once tried—impossible! There is nothing to add. Nor is there to this other line :—

    ' O pasteur, Hespêrus à l'occident s'allume !' [1]

The melancholy of the hour, the clear evening, the shining star and the pastoral life, it is all there; why seek for anything further? "

" It is true," said I, " that that kind of stanza, the single stanza in which a whole poem seems to be condensed, is sufficient unto itself and disdains rhyme. I have composed one myself, very absurd, but who could find a rhyme to add to it ?

    ' Je suis le nautonier des océans lunaires !' [2]

The Italian poet, Gualdo, has quoted this line somewhere as an epigraph, in order to silence his contemporaries and make them search for its origin."

Villiers suddenly began to rummage in his pockets, and, after an agitated search, he drew out some very crumpled sheets of paper.

[1] O shepherd, Vesper kindles at the west !
[2] I am the boatman of the lunar seas !

"Let us be serious again," said he, "let us be practical and prosaic. Here is my article upon the exposition : it is finished."

"What ! " cried I, "have you not sent it yet ? It will be too late : the opening of the exposition is an old story now: they will not wish to publish it."

"Oh, if you could see with what fine little touches it has all been refreshed ! In the first place, I have changed the title, which is now : 'Munich during the Exposition.' Really the article isn't bad, listen to this : "

And he read :—

"The halls of the Crystal Palace are filled to overflowing, the French envoys are rudely bumped by the enormous boxes. At the exposition the paintings reach to the very cornices, and there is even talk of hanging some delayed canvases in the restaurant opposite, notably the *Casseur de Pierres* of Courbet. We must add, however, that Courbet has also sent here a magnificent landscape, in which the water is so natural and so deep that it makes one dream dreams. That, and the *Fauconnier* of Couture, are the pictures that we love best in the French salon, in spite of our lack of sympathy for the realistic school.

" The Germans, when they see Courbet's paintings, say, ' A painter as good as he is rough, he sees like a peasant and paints like a professor, which is saying a great deal,' they add laughing."

" Here I interpolate a sentence," said Villiers. " ' It is late to speak of the exposition,' and then I go on to speak of it all the same :

" One must also mention some exquisite grisailles of Ramberg, the *Saint Joseph* of Gysis, portraits by Lenbach, landscapes by Zwangauer, the German Daubigny, some academic sepias of Kaulbach on subjects drawn from Wagner's operas, and *The woman in the velvet Gown*, of Herr Canon, a young Austrian painter of incomparable talent. It is thought that *The Banquet of Phaton* of Herr Anselm Feuerbach, will have the medal of honour. It is great work, truly, and since Peter Cornelius, nothing better has been done in Germany. So art is in a flourishing condition.

" I am going to slip a new sentence in there," said Villiers. " ' Let us now leave the exposition, with its already old news, and take a promenade through the city.' "

And he continued his reading :—

" We love Munich, but not everyone is of our
opinion. It is true that Munich is rather lacking in
police officers, that *Les Pompiers de Nanterre* is not
sung here, that we notice an absence of assaults,
swindlings and murders that is truly desolating
for the future of this capital. On the other hand,
we have seen magnificent theatres where Goethe
is played, we have visited museums which contain
treasures of art and of genius, we have seen monu-
ments in the purest Greek style, great gardens
like the Bois de Boulogne, immense cafés where
one is served by pretty girls whom no one dreams
of chaffing beyond reason, except, perhaps, some
passing wags who have only their trouble for
their pains.

" We have climbed up inside ' The Bavaria,'
the enormous bronze statue which towers above
the city, and through the eyes of which six people
are able to see before them the sweep of land
extending to the mountains of the Tyrol. We
have visited the hall of the portraits of beautiful
women of the country, where one imagines oneself
in a sort of Montyon Gallery of love, and where,
if her nose be of an heroic cast, the daughter of
a shoemaker may find herself side by side with

the daughter of a princess. The king, Ludwig I.,
who lodged in his palace this ingenuous display
of Germanic beauty, loved all pretty women;
and the good Bavarians recount that at his death
the following scene must have taken place at
the gate of Heaven :

" Rap ! Rap ! "

" ' Who is there ? ' asks St Peter.'

" ' It is I, Ludwig, King of Bavaria ! '

" ' One moment,' replies the blessed Apostle.
Then he shouts in a voice of thunder : ' Get the
eleven thousand virgins out of the way quick !
Here is Ludwig of Bavaria just arriving ! ' '

" But we must not laugh too much about
that king who, in the place of military glory, has
bequeathed to his people schools where the children
are taught to develop a lofty and noble character."

" That is very good, Villiers, but you must
not read any more," cried I, interrupting him.
" Let us hurry to the post, there is still time
before the evening collection. Let us send the
article at once, the more you allow the time to
pass, the less chance there is of its being published,
for, in spite of your conciliatory sentence, present
time does not wait."

X

After the tiresome incident of the Hôtel des Quatre Saisons, when Villiers had removed his shoes before a noble audience, we sulked at the social world, refused its invitations, and when there was nothing very interesting at the theatres, we loved to gather in the evening at the house of Franz Servais.

Servais, who made very frequent visits to Munich, had there a large apartment on the ground floor, in a quarter a little away from the centre. He possessed a piano, around which we passed many delightful hours, thanks to the unwearied kindness of Hans Richter, who played us fragments from the *Rheingold* to initiate us a little into the work which we were so soon to have the happiness of seeing represented.

Servais had not held any resentment against Villiers; he quite understood now that he had done what he believed was necessary, and they had become good companions and were on the best of terms.

Sometimes we amused ourselves by playing charades. It was undoubtedly I who proposed this kind of diversion, of which I was very fond. It was a pastime that had pleased my father, and with which, at Neuilly, he had often enlivened the Thursdays at home of the Rue de Longchamp.

From the first, Servais showed a remarkable aptitude. He was always ready with something opportune, something unexpected, and he was never deterred by the fear of producing comical effects. Villiers, great actor as he was! declared himself to be incapable of improvising two sentences, so reserved for himself the honour of guessing the word of the charade. Schuré requested to be allowed to hold the office of the public—a rather abstracted public—while Scheffer and his dog, which never left him, were both very attentive. As for Richter, he consented to-appear in the rôle of a mute personage, so mute even, that upon one occasion when representing a sick man, he allowed the brilliantine to be poured into his mouth without a protest, in order not to spoil the effect.

How did the lady of many names, who ought to have had something else to do, take it into her head to announce to the whole city the way in which we passed our evenings ? It always seemed to be known. One evening when we had had supper at the Café Maximilian, just as we started to go out, we saw several carriages roll up and stop one after the other in front of the Café. Before we had time to think about it, the Countess Muchanoff alighted from the first coach and entered hastily.

" At last you are found ! " cried she, " you have become very elusive, you are never at your apartments, you never come when one invites you, so we decided to look for you everywhere. For the last hour we have been going to all the beer-gardens, all the restaurants in Munich ; this is the very last one."

We were a little disconcerted. Villiers had made a show of running away, but the retreat was cut off, the doors of the other carriages opened, ladies and gentlemen, who figured in the elegant society which had been present at the disastrous fête, spread out over the much be-glorified side-walk.

" It is very wrong of you to be so exclusive," continued Madame Muchanoff, " to organise charming evening parties, without letting anyone know ! Now that we have discovered you, we

shall take you all away with us. Come, come,
you must do some charades, we are all so curious
to see that ! ”

" Charades ! ”

How did they know ? . . . and did they really
imagine that we would proceed to play at charades
in the city ?

" But, dear lady——” said I to her, " it was only
among ourselves and as one would play at
children's games, that we amused ourselves so ;
we should lose all our spontaneity if we under-
took to be serious about it.”

They begged and they insisted, but we remained
firm and unmoved. We asserted that we considered them all as our guests, that we ought to
receive and entertain them, and that they must
excuse us for not being able to do it in a Café.

At this moment someone opened for us an
empty room, turned on the lights, and all these
gay people, very much pleased, went in there,
followed by the surprised and admiring gaze of
the public. The ladies loosened their evening
wraps and revealed their bare shoulders and light
costumes. The men were in evening coats.

Many of the persons present we hardly knew,

and at first we were a little ill at ease. But
someone ordered tea, someone else champagne,
the women lighted their Russian cigarettes,
as slender as toothpicks, and the momentary
awkwardness vanished. Count von Berghem, a
man with very fascinating manners, of whom
I know nothing more than his name, entered
into a discussion with Schuré and Servais upon
the analogies which exist between the Gods of
Edda, from whom Wagner has taken his heroes,
and the Gods of Olympus, between Wotan and
Jupiter.

The Countess Muchanoff seemed determined to
reconquer Villiers, who escaped from her as long
as possible, but she made such gracious advances
to him, she expressed such a lively admiration
for his talent and his mind, that he regained all
his assurance.

In fact, this rather unusual overture, this
unexpected invasion, became a very charming
and cordial event. The conclusion of the episode
revealed Villiers' character : he was no longer
crestfallen at having seated himself upon the
piano and allowed his feet to dangle, he only
regretted that he did not have his Maltese cross

in his pocket on this occasion, so that he could pin it to his waistcoat.

XI

Our friends wished very much to show us the model of the Semper theatre that Wagner had charged us to go and see, and which was very seldom shown. A sort of basement in the Royal Residence served as a place of concealment for this very pretty miniature theatre—modelled in plaster, and standing upon a large table of white wood. Greatly interested, we circled about the little edifice, the plan of which is so rational and so well adapted to its purpose—and it saddened us to think of Wagner's frustrated hopes and bitter disappointment at having to give up his plan for constructing a model theatre.

Who could have foretold that, seven years later, thanks to the unflagging faith of the royal friend, we should see it rise up, triumphant, upon the hill at Bayreuth ?

XII

Richard Wagner, while in Munich, had been for a long time the neighbour of Count Friedrich von

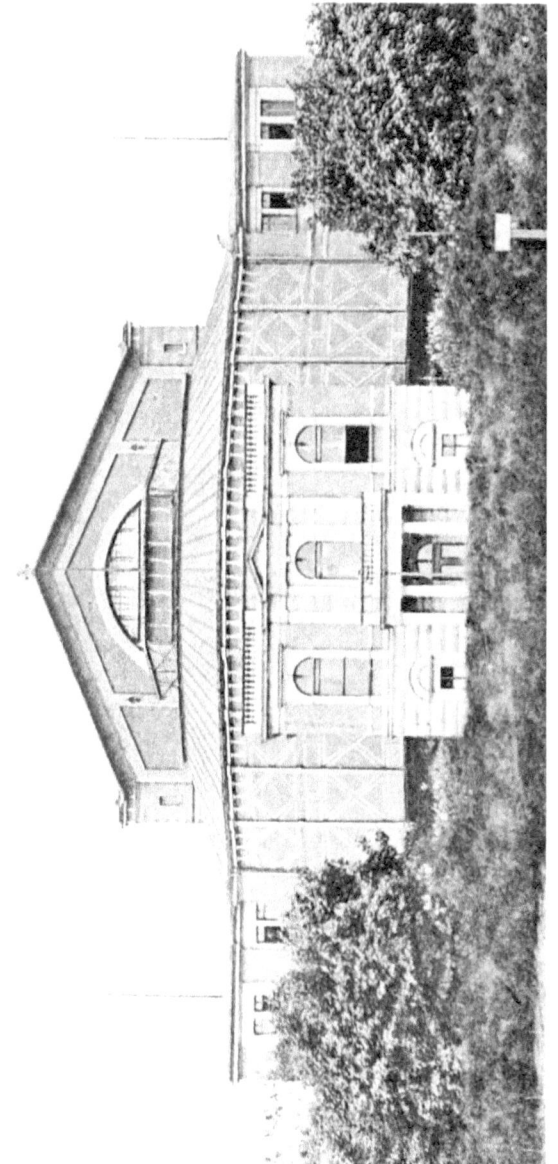

WAGNER'S THEATRE AT BAYREUTH.

Schack, and there was a warm friendship between them. I was commissioned to remind Richter not to forget to invite the Count to the dress rehearsal of the *Rheingold,* and I had promised, also, to pay a visit to his famous collection of paintings.

This Count von Schack was a writer of some celebrity—his " History of Literature and Dramatic Art in Spain " Wagner esteemed very highly ; he knew Arabic, Persian, Sanscrit, and had translated, among others, the " Book of the Kings " of Ferdousi. At one time the Master contemplated a musical drama founded upon one of the episodes of this work ; he was also tempted by a legend contained in " The Voices of the Ganges," a collection also translated by Schack.

As to his museum, the public reviled more than they praised it ; they even went so far as to call it the " Krausteum " (so true it is that philanthropy engenders ingratitude)—because of the things gathered in by this millionaire, who believed himself to be doing right in ordering pictures from poor artists from whom no one else had ever ordered !

L

As a matter of fact, the collection included not a few horrors and some very beautiful works.

The copies of the great masters, from Lenbach's brush, for example, seemed to me very remarkable. They recalled to me a commission for this artist, with which Cosima had charged me, and I decided to go at once to his studio, which was near the Schack gallery.

Lenbach had a delicate, rather crafty face, the sharp look of the hunter, a short, red-brown beard and a one-sided smile.

He showed me some delicious portraits of children which he was just finishing, he made me admire some authentic and very beautiful canvases of the old masters which were in his possession, among others, a sketch by Rubens and a splendid portrait of Francis I. by Titian.

This is what I had come to say to him :—

" It is absolutely necessary that you should paint the portrait of Richard Wagner, it is a disgrace to Germany that no artist of worth has yet attempted it. Madame Cosima sends the order to you, and leaves you free to fix your own price."

" I will undertake the work with the greatest

pleasure," said Lenbach, " and I wish no further
payment than the honour of having done it if
I should succeed."

" That is indeed worthy of you," said I, holding
out my hand to him, " but Cosima will doubtless
feel differently, you must discuss that question
with her."

" There is another portrait which I should also
very much love to do, and it is yours."

" My portrait !   You could find time for that ? "

" I could do it at once, I beg you to allow me
to do it."

O, careless youth !   Many times Lenbach spoke
again of this portrait, but the idea of posing
wearied me and I evaded the appointments.
The poignant regret that I now feel is surely a
sufficient punishment.

XIII

The rehearsals of the *Rheingold* with orchestra
had commenced !   Wagner had made it a point
that his friends should be allowed to be present
at the last one before the dress rehearsal.   This
prospect filled us with joy.

Richter, however, seemed to be anxious.   Could

anything be going wrong ? The singers were of
the first rank and full of enthusiasm, the members
of the orchestra were, without a doubt, the best
in the world,—but there was also the management
of the theatre, which laboured secretly at the
staging of the work. What would this staging
be like, without the suggestions of the Master,
carried on by a management that was hostile
to him, and looking out only for itself ?   Incredible as it may appear, it is true that the men
who directed and managed the theatre, to which
Wagner brought glory and profit, were hostile
to Wagner.

And yet the manager, Perfall, had been
appointed solely at the recommendation of the
Master, whom he had solicited with a servile
insistence, swearing that he would have no other
object except to devote himself to him and to
his interests, with all his heart and all his ability.
As soon as he was appointed, with an unparalleled
treachery, he had betrayed the one to whom he
owed his position, and hindered in a thousand
ways the production of the *Meistersinger*.

Nor could one depend very much more upon
the Court Counsellor, Lorenz von Düfflipp, in-

termediary between the Palace and the theatre, who, in spite of his obsequious flatteries of Wagner, was secretly adverse to him, and hand in hand with the management.

Fruitless reprisals indeed, but we called him " Tartufflipp," [1] and his title of " Hofrath " changed itself for us into " Chaussetrappe." [2]

This counsellor, secretary to the king, had replaced Pfistmeister, the messenger who had carried the good news to Wagner from Ludwig II., and who was now, also, one of his most implacable adversaries.

" Tartufflipp," with his prepossessing face, was badly built, high-shouldered, even hump-backed —and the report ran that his hump was greatly increased by the Wagnerian theatre project, which having juggled away, he had concealed there.

What could result from all these artful under-hand dealings ? Already they had written me from Tribschen that the costumes, according to the sketches sent to the Master, were hideous and would have to be re-made. Someone had conceived the idea of building up great scaffolds

[1] Hypocrite.   [2] Trap-door.

of gold upon the heads of the Gods, without remembering that in this opera, where gold is discovered, it ought not to appear until after Alberich had plundered and forged it. Would attention be paid to the author's suggestions ? In that which pertained to the staging was there not all to be feared, considering that the only beings upon whom it depended were spiteful and incapable ?

Decidedly, Richter's anxiety explained itself and extended to us.

XIV

At last the time had come ! The last rehearsal but one was about to begin. How mysterious and imposing was the empty and dimly lighted theatre ! It appeared immense, almost like a cathedral, the stage all bathed in a blue haze, produced, no doubt, by some reflection of the outside daylight, for it was then three o'clock in the afternoon.

Only a very few had been accorded the favour of being present at this rehearsal, which was without stage scenery or costumes.

Liszt was there. His tall dark silhouette loomed up from the orchestra stalls. I hastened to salute the Great Man, now become the friend, and I asked if he would permit me to remain near him during the rehearsal, that he might explain to me some things in the opera, the score of which I did not sufficiently know. The permission was very graciously accorded.

Now the musicians began to arrive and to take their places! How solemn and almost religious was the emotion we felt!

" For very many years I have waited for this moment," said Liszt, " and I have feared, indeed, that it would never come. . . . If you but knew the miseries, the wrecked and perished hopes despite which this work has germed and flowered! I have seen it all and I have suffered too because of it. I do not know how Wagner has been able to preserve his divine inspiration intact. He seems to me like a traveller who bore a cup full of water through the midst of a whirlwind without being forced to spill a single drop. But even in harbour, you see, he finds no shelter. . . . During his exile he was for many years the only German who had not heard *Lohengrin*. To - day, the tones of his great orchestra revealing his new work to the world, will sound for the first time

and he will not hear them.   Ah, what a ransom
ought to be paid to genius ! ''

Now came Richter, pale and grave, and mounted
to his desk.

We were hardly a dozen listeners in the dark
audience hall.   I caught a glimpse of the blond,
almost white locks of Servais, and I divined the
form of Edouard Schuré beside him.   I also saw
a shadow, climbing over the orchestra chairs :
it was Villiers hastening to seat himself farther
back, in order to be quite alone, quite undistracted.

They drew the curtain before the stage.   Richter
gave two or three quick blows on the desk, then
with a serious and proud gesture raised his baton.

And now a deep, muffled tone rises from the
orchestra, it vibrates almost imperceptibly in the
lowest depths of the scale, indistinct, without
form, it trembles in a limpid motion, then seems
to dilate, to spread out, a slow sweet gliding
movement floats up and loses itself, soon another
ripples up along the same path and floats away,
as one wave follows another.

Very soon these musical waves swell out and
follow each other continuously upward ; from
above spheres of light seem to fall, spreading and

diffusing like drops of milk in clear water. The
curtain is drawn to reveal mysterious abysses
seen through the blue transparency of the Rhine.
On the stage there is nothing but a confused
shadow, but how clearly the imagination inspired
by the music, evokes the picture ! Better, perhaps, than could the scenery itself.

Now a gentle undulation sways the tranquil
water and suddenly a crystal voice resounds
through the crystal fluid, a nymph glides from
the heights and swims below, stirring the water
to new motion. The words of her song form
sliding syllables :

Weïa ! Waga ! Woge, du Welle,
Walle zur Wiege ! Wagala Weïa
Wallala Weiala Weïa !

And she sways about the reef, at the summit of
which dimly gleams the vein of gold ; then another
daughter of the Rhine plunges from the heights
and joyously pursues her flying sister. But the
voice of a third undine chides them both as she,
laughing, sings :

Heila Weïa !
Wildes Geschwister !
Des Goldes Schlaf
Hütet ihr schlecht ;
Besser bewacht
Des schlummernden Bett
Sonst büsst ihr beide das Spiel !

Then she in her turn dives below, and these gracious dwellers of the Rhine swim and frolic, upborne by the harmonious waves of music, around the prophetic rock where sleeps the imprisoned gold, untouched and virgin still.

On this occasion the Rhine maidens are standing quietly upon the platform in walking costumes and straw hats, but they can hardly be seen in the obscurity and, without interfering with our imaginings they lend their fresh and limpid voices to the forms the poet has created.

Now comes a heavy and jarring rhythm, and from the most obscure depths of the river, slowly emerges a strange dwarf, with white hair and long white beard braided into one strand. He climbs along the slippery rocks. The music expresses his struggles, as he complains of the painful ascent, alliterating his words :

> Garstig glatter
> Glitschriger Glimmer !
> Wie gleit ich aus !

His eager look follows the undines in their charming play, and, unable to reach them, he calls to them :

> He, He ! Ihr Nicker !
> Wie seid ihr niedlich
> Neidliches Volk !

Aus Nibelheim's Nacht
Naht' ich euch gern,
Neigtet ihr euch zu mir.

The Rhine maidens, frightened, cluster about the rock :

" Hütet das Gold !
Vater warnte
Von solchem Feind."

" What dost thou seek, thou who comest up from below ? "

" Wie scheint im Schimmer
Ihr hell und schön
Wie gern umschlänge
Der schlanken eine mein Arm
Schlüpfte hold sie herab ! "

" Nun lach ich der Furcht
Der Feind ist verliebt."

And the frolicsome undines dive from the rocks, pursuing, enticing, tempting the ardent dwarf, who, in a passionate fury, leaps from rock to rock, trying to catch one or another. But the elusive maidens always evade him, slipping away, and as he falls back, breathless and angry, the clear notes of their mocking laughter float back to him.

But to-day, in the pleasure of reviving these memories, I must not fall into the error of describing the *Rheingold.* When I first heard it in Munich in the solemn stillness of the dark theatre, it was like the virgin metal gleaming in the sunlight at the summit of the rock, for the first time revealed to the world, while now, like gold which has passed through the mint, it is known to all.

This first part of the Tetralogy, which is the prologue, was not divided into acts. Its four tableaux were given without interruption. The scenes were shifted in full view of the audience to the accompaniment of the orchestra. The performance lasted for more than two hours, and yet, even at this first hearing when all the faculties of attention were taxed to the utmost, one did not experience any fatigue; the architectural outline of the drama was so simple and clear cut, the music evoked with so much certainty the different phases, or so to speak, the elementaries of the work, and individualized them in themes and rhythms of such extraordinary beauty.

Only one passage seemed to me difficult to understand, the one where Wotan, in the face of the treasure forged by the Nibelungen which he has just ravished from them, is, according to the

text, " struck by a high thought." At this
moment is heard for the first and only time, the
" Leit-motif " of the sword, that sword called
" Nothung " which is to play such an important
role in the following works, but which, when the
theme enters which symbolises it, is not designated
by any phrase or gesture. Liszt, whom I questioned about it, agreed with me that here was
an obscurity, and that Wagner would have noticed
it if he had been present at the rehearsals. Later,
I spoke to the Master himself with regard to this
point, and he remarked that the observation was
a very just one, and that he would take advantage
of it. After that, a sword was added to the
treasure of the Nibelungen ; Wotan discovered
and brandished it at the moment when the theme
was introduced.

We were all carried away by enthusiasm when
the Gods, walking across the valley on the rainbow,
entered Walhalla and the curtain fell. Richter,
flushed with emotion, was surrounded, acclaimed.
Liszt embraced and complimented him warmly.
The singers were also praised, and the musicians
of the orchestra who had so admirably fulfilled
their glorious task.

After having escorted Liszt to his carriage, still filled with elation that was not to be calmed we set out, all together, to take possession of the Café Maximilian. Instead of ordering supper, we asked for pens and paper, and each one of us wrote to Richard Wagner, expressing to him all the admiration and delight which his new masterpiece had inspired in us, and thanking him for having accorded us the great favour of hearing it before the general public, and even alas, before he himself had heard it.

XV

It was the 25th of August, anniversary day of the birth of King Ludwig II. Munich was adorned with flags, and its regiments marched in full dress uniforms of sky blue. We had heard one of their bands play before the Royal Palace the very " Huldigung-Marsch "—which I had so laboriously deciphered at four hands with Wagner. The King was not in Munich, but would come in time to be present at the dress rehearsal of the *Rheingold*, which was to take place on Friday the 27th of August—two days later.

Ludwig II., who was adored by his people, did

not seek for ovations. On the contrary, he avoided them as often as possible, and thereby greatly disappointed the Bavarian people, who were always eager to see him and were so rarely gratified!

It appeared indeed, that all the young girls of the kingdom, and even perhaps, all the women, were in love with their youthful and charming sovereign; but he was haughty and reserved by nature, and in the wonderful locations which he had chosen for his castles he lived almost alone, surrounded by the splendours of art and the beauties of Nature.

This, however, did not prevent him from fulfilling his duties as king; he had according to custom inaugurated the International Exposition of Painting, and had left the city the same day. Very few would have the opportunity of seeing him when he should return to hear the work of his great friend.

I, too, was born on the 25th of August, the day of St Ludwig the king, so it was also my fête-day. I had told Cosima this fact because of my vain-glory in possessing something in common with the royal archangel. To my great surprise, she remembered it and sent me a charming parasol, of a new model, which they called, "Sea-side parasol," the novelty consisting in the fact that it could also be used as a cane. So, in promenading through Maximilianstrasse, I liked better to lean upon my parasol than to open it and shelter myself from the sun.

Many pilgrims were to be seen in Munich, come from all sides to hear the *Rheingold.* Among them were pointed out to us, Madame Pauline Viardot, Saint-Saëns, Tourguenef, Baron von Leon, manager of the theatre at Weimar, and many others whom I have forgotten.

We were all very nervous and excited. Only two days more! Would everything be ready? Hans Richter could not conceal his disquietude, so many things about the conduct of the manager seemed to him to be ambiguous.

"Perfall will not allow anything to be seen of his stage arrangements," said he, "but he has the expression of a traitor."

"Perfall, Perfide!"

One would have said that the labours of the Cyclops were taking place behind the walls of the long closed theatre. There were rumours of

steam engines, hoisted upon the stage by means
of lifting machines and pulleys. For what
purpose ? Truly it was very terrifying ; what
would come of all this mystery ?

In any case Richter was sure of his orchestra.
It was he, who like St Christoper with the child
Jesus, would bear the whole weight of the under-
taking upon his robust shoulders.

XVI

At last it was the 27th of August and we entered
the theatre.

A crowd of spectators were gathered about
the entrance and before the Royal Palace.
They must have known that the apartments in
the palace communicated directly with the royal
box, and that no one could see the King pass
or know when he entered the theatre, so it could
only have been the irresistible attraction of walls
behind which something is happening, that held
all those loungers there.

The theatre was brilliantly lighted, although
nearly empty. The hundred or so persons whom
the King had seen fit to invite were scattered
through the house and were hardly noticeable.

M

The side boxes and a few rows of the orchestra chairs were to be used on this occasion. The dress circle and the boxes facing the stage, in the midst of which the royal box filled so large a space, were shut off.

I gazed at the sumptuous decorations of that loge, the frame to which the picture was as yet lacking, but which would hold in a few moments the so longed-for figure of the young sovereign. It would be our first glimpse of him, of that being who inspired in us such a profound sympathy, of him who radiated the glory of having been able to correct an error of destiny, and diminish the shame that humanity would endure for having failed to recognise Genius.

The blue velvet draperies with their rich folds held back by cords of gold, the crown and coat of arms, lozenged in blue and silver, and borne by the rampant lions, which signified in the language of heraldry "up and ready," these only caught the light, and the royal box itself was like a grotto of darkness.

All of a sudden the King was there, sparkling in the obscurity like a star emerged from the mist. His youthful visage gave us a delightful surprise.

We had not imagined him like that, at once
feminine and headstrong, ingenuous and arrogant.
In contrast to the very black locks of his hair,
which, standing up from his forehead, seemed to
guard him like a wave of flame, his skin was of a
warm, almost, dusky pallor, and a singular expression of energy contrasted strongly with the
delicate modelling of his features ; but one was
instantly fascinated by the extraordinary splendour
of those eyes, blue-green as the sea, fringed with
long black lashes, eyes profound, ecstatic. . . .
" Nothing is able to give any idea of the magic
of that glance," said the Master.

The king advanced to the front of the box.
His tall form dominated the house for an instant :
then he seated himself. Very soon the lights
were turned down and the vision vanished. But
Hans Richter did not yet give the signal to the
orchestra. The footlights were lighted, but before
the curtain was drawn a man slipped out before
it from a corner of the stage.

Perfall, the manager ! What could he wish to
say ?

After many bowings and scrapings, with his
hand on his heart he spoke, he implored " the

indulgence of the select public before whom he had the honour. . . . In spite of the best will in the world, of long conscientious efforts . . . insurmountable difficulties of scenery . . . effects impossible to realise. . . . It had been necessary to give up the idea of attaining perfection, and to be content with what could be done, regret, chagrin . . . but there is no flying without wings. . . ."

The presence of the king kept back all marked demonstration: yet even that could not stifle the indignant murmur that followed Perfall, when, after fresh cringings, he disappeared behind the curtain.

Richter struck angrily upon his desk, as if he were hitting the back of the traitor. The low note began its muffled vibration, the prelude commenced: but we no longer listened in the religious absorption of the other day, we were afraid to see the curtain drawn aside . . . and at that moment it was drawn.

One was disappointed at the very first glance; no sign of the green shadows, of the humid and troubled depths which we had expected to see, only very dry rocks of moulded paper, resting without mystery, upon the boards of the stage.

A frightful oil lamp, suspended from the highest moulding was supposed to represent " the gold of the Rhine." It only recalled the lantern which is placed, by night, at the top of a street obstruction. . . . The crystalline voice unrolled its clear melody, but at this point, a mannikin with dangling arms and hair hanging before its face, intended for an undine, was precipitated, head first, from above and, half way down, remained suspended, balancing from the end of a string. At the moment when the other voices were heard, other images of the same nature fell from above and oscillated in the deplorable attitudes of the drowned. Soon after, the mannikins were drawn back, and the true singers, standing upon supports, half concealed by the jutting out of the paper rocks, appeared and agitated their arms to represent swimming. Then they went away, and the puppet Rhine maidens returned and capered desperately about the smoking lamp.

What absurdity! They would not dare to present anything so bad at the Punch and Judy show of the Champs-Elysées.

After the scene-shifting, of an unbelievable awkwardness, a very little Walhalla, like a castle of cards, was to be seen upon a miniature mountain. Wotan had the appearance of a wayfarer who sleeps in the open air. As soon as he began to sing however, the magnificent voice of Betz made one willing to forget all else, one no longer saw the ridiculous landscape, and as the mechanical difficulties were over for the time, one could listen to the scenes that followed up to the moment of the descent to the Nibelheim.

At that point the management took its revenge.

A frightful and continuous hissing suddenly drowned both the voices and the orchestra. What in the world could it be ? At first one was terrified, but heavy clouds of white vapour soon enveloped the scene and all was explained : the famous machines ! A red Bengal fire, lighted too late, coloured those clouds, which were supposed to escape from the subterranean kingdom of the Nibelungen forgers.

When, a little later, Alberich should have donned the magic helmet in order to take the form of the dragon, he very simply walked off at the wings and the dragon entered by the same path, then the dragon went back, and the man returned.

The steam engine was not employed in the last scene; at the moment when Donner assembled the clouds and let loose the storm, the hissing might have helped to represent the whistlings of the tempest. At that time, however, what seemed to be blocks of granite descended from the freize and moved to the right and the left without knowing where to stop. The Gods climbed painfully up after the storm, and beheld, added to the scenery of before, a large bridge in white linen, which crossed the valley and reached to the other side, erasing and overwhelming the tiny Walhalla.

Toward this whiteness the Gods direct their steps. Then that must be the rainbow over which they are to pass. Yes, of course it is, for now a prismatic light, thrown from a lantern, runs distractedly over the lower end of the linen, onto Wotan's nose, everywhere it ought not to be, and never reaches the bridge, massive and white, for which it is intended.

At length the curtain falls, the orchestra is silent. Richter, red with wrath, throws down his baton; the usually amiable Richter looks positively fierce.

"I will not direct such a *Rheingold*," cried he, "it is war between you and me, Herr Manager!" And to us he said, "Wait for me at the Café Maximilian, we must join together in forewarning the Master."

XVII

The first presentation of the *Rheingold* was billed for Sunday, the 29th August, two days later. Under the circumstances, it must be prevented from taking place.

If the stage settings had been simply mediocre, it might have been possible to resign oneself and count upon the splendour of the work to make one forget the inadequacy of its plastic realisation : but here there was too much of the grotesque, too many things that made one laugh, the bad faith and malevolence were too evident : there must be a protest so violent as to prevent the accomplishment of the sacrilege.

After we were all reunited in our usual place at the Café Maximilian, the conference was not a long one. Richter had had a stormy interview with Perfall.

" Postpone the representation," said Richter.

" The representation will take place on Sunday,"
replied Perfall.

" We shall see ! "

" We shall see ! "

" And he *will* see," added Richter. " My
resolution is taken, but I did not wish to announce
it before asking Wagner's advice. Quick. Let
us get to business ! "

He wrote a dispatch in German, and we wrote
the following in French :

" Master, the orchestra, under the direction of
Hans Richter, was admirable. The singers deserve
the highest praise. The scenery and the stage
mechanism are absurd, ridiculous, impossible."
And, while someone hurried off with the telegrams,
I wrote a long letter to Wagner, giving him a
detailed account of the spectacle at which we had
just been present and concerning which we were
still trembling with indignation.

Betz also wrote to the Master, who would
receive the dispatches the same evening and the
letters the following morning.

We awaited the replies in the greatest impatience.

The first telegram which arrived the next day was for Richter :

" Will they really offer me such an insult as to give my work to-morrow ? "

At the theatre the *Rheingold* was still announced. Richter showed Wagner's dispatch to Perfall, but he paid no attention to it, and persisted in his determination to give the work upon the date for which it was billed.

I received a letter from Tribschen in which Wagner said that he thanked me for the vivid description I had sent him of this disaster, that he had telegraphed to the King asking him to suspend the representations, that he had telegraphed to Betz begging him to refuse to sing under such conditions.

On Sunday morning Richter went for a last time to see the Director, and said to him :

" The representation of the *Rheingold* will not take place this evening, because I will not conduct the work against the wish of its author."

" You will not conduct it this evening, nor any other evening," cried Perfall—" as you are no longer Capellmeister to the Royal Theatre."

And pale with rage, he signed the dismissal of Hans Richter.

But at least they could not play the *Rheingold* that evening. Better that the sea should swallow one man than the whole ship.

A strip was pasted across the bills, postponing the performance to the following Thursday. The management sought for a new leader of orchestra, there was a mad rush about Munich, where many Capellmeisters had come to hear the *Rheingold*

All those whom they solicited, stole away, leaving the city precipitately; not one of them cared to incur the disapproval of the composer by conducting the work against his will.

On Monday another letter brought the news that Wagner had written at length to the King, explaining to him in all its details, the affair of the *Rheingold* and begging him to postpone again the performance announced for Thursday to the following Sunday. If it were in accordance with the King's wishes, Wagner would himself go to Munich to re-instal Richter at the desk and to reorganize the scenes as much as possible.

The Master had submitted the same conditions to the management of the theatre the day before, and had received a telegram, come out of the Counsellor's hump, to the effect that the conditions were granted and that they only prayed him to allow them to give the representation on Thursday.

Wagner telegraphed in answer to that :—

" I await a response from the King to a letter sent off to-day."

But on this same evening of Monday, the 30th August, Richter received a dispatch from Wagner which announced his own arrival for the following day. He had not the patience to wait for the King's answer. He would come in the strictest secrecy, no one was to know where he would stay, and, we must understand, it was necessary to guard the secret most carefully.

XVIII

" Alte Pferdestrasse, Wagner, who has just arrived in Munich, is there, come to-night, after dark."

We had all gathered at Franz Servais' house to await the news, when this note was brought to me and put into " the right hands " with much mystery. It was not signed, but Richter had written it.

" Richard Wagner here ! " We expected him, yet now we were surprised and troubled that he had come, even though in answer to our call. . . . What if some misfortune should grow out of this incident ! . . . On the contrary, all would come right now that the Master was here, his presence would work miracles.

" Alte Pferdestrasse," said Servais, " Wagner has gone to Scheffer's home : what an honour ! "

" Who is this Scheffer, then ? " asked Villiers, " always so silent and buried in his beard ? One cannot make him out at all."

" He is correspondent of some small German papers, according to his own account, but, I believe also an office-holder. Certainly he is a good Wagnerian, and that ought to suffice for us."

" His dog is also that," replied Villiers, " for he only comes when one whistles the serenade of Beckmesser."

" Where is the Alte Pferdestrasse ? " I asked.

" In a very quiet part of the city, but it is not easy to find—" said Servais. " We will take you there and wait for you, since you only are invited to see the Master. . . ."

It was still daylight when we left Servais' house and sauntered slowly along, in order not to have the air of conspirators. We asked ourselves if Wagner really ran any risks, in coming to Munich. He was not really exiled, only morally so, by his own resolution not to go there. What had he to fear? The public was eager for his works: the price of seats in the theatre doubled when they were played, and the house was always full. Were his enemies still so implacable, and what could they do?

We stopped before the theatre to read the posters and wonder what Perfall was plotting. The *Rheingold* was announced for Thursday, two days later. The management was stubborn: nevertheless it would have to concede one point; who would conduct the orchestra, if not Richter?

We went on, and were nearly lost in a labyrinth of small deserted streets with grass growing between the pavingstones, with little, low houses and small gardens.

" Alte Pferdestrasse." At last we found it; my companions stopped at the corner of the street and Franz Servais pointed out the house of the greatly envied Scheffer. The entrance door was closed and I knew that porters were not usual in the Munich houses. I could see the shining brass of three little bells, but it had grown very dark, and I could not succeed in making out the name of the resident or the number of the floor engraved under each. Leaving it to chance, I rang the middle one! Chance served me this time, for Scheffer himself came to let me in. We mounted a narrow dimly-lighted staircase to the first floor.

As soon as we passed the threshold, I saw Wagner, at the end of the second room, seated on an old sofa.

Then I suddenly remembered Tribschen, the superb frame which seemed so fitting a place for the Master. I thought how at this hour, between the high mountains, deep shadows brooded over the dear home, which no longer held his presence, and anxiety possessed the heart of her, who in spirit followed the absent one.

How strange it was to find Wagner in this narrow and shabby setting! Yet, because it held him, one was no longer conscious of the restrictions : he transformed all that surrounded him.

" Well, dear friend," he said to me, " here are the Misérabilites in full force ! I do not regret that you should have been a witness of the occurrence that has brought me here, for there are some things that one could never believe, unless one had seen them."

" But the King, what does the King say ? "

" Ah, I imagine that he feigns to ignore the fiasco, and does not wish to be drawn into it. They have probably persuaded him that it is impossible to do better, or to make the stage effects realistic : he wishes to enjoy again the pleasure he had in hearing the music and probably said to his subordinates :

" ' Arrange as well as you can, but give me another representation of the *Rheingold* as soon as possible.' "

" How could he understand, after having put at the disposition of the Director the enormous sum of sixty thousand florins, and commanding him not to spare time in obtaining a perfect result, how could he imagine such bad will and malevolence in those whom he employs ? "

" But now that you are here, Master, all will
be different."

" No, alas ! The first representation is still
billed for Thursday. The King wishes it and I
am not willing to oppose him. You know that
all my new works belong to him, in exchange for
the yearly indemnity which he grants me. As
soon as any score is completed, I send it to him
and he has the right to dispose of it as he pleases.
This time, I am protesting inwardly, but mutely,
against the fragmentary representations of the
Tetralogy. But how can I feel any ill-will toward
the King for his impatience ? Toward him who
has endeavoured in every way to put through
the theatre project which would have permitted
the bringing out of my work as a whole ? He
cannot resign himself to waiting, as I should have
liked to have him wait, for the better times, and
he wishes to see, at least, the representations of
parts of my work. I can only submit myself.
And all this creates rather a delicate situation.
He is vexed that I do not accept the situation
as he has done, and that I refuse to direct the
studies of the *Rheingold,* and I am grieved that
he exercises his right to have them represented.

N

But, like my mute protestation, so his blame is unspoken. Nothing greater than that could come to trouble a friendship such as ours; it is only a squall, which dulls for a moment the surface of a beautiful lake."

" Then Master, what will you be able to do here before Thursday ? "

" First and above all, I wish to re-instal Richter at the desk and I have asked for a rehearsal to-morrow, for myself alone, when I shall endeavour to improve whatever I can, to correct the greatest faults, if it is possible to do it. I owe this effort to my honour as an artist, to the devotion of our matchless Richter and of my interpreters ; I owe it to my friends ; this conviction has made me break the promise that I made to myself, not to come here, or mix in any way in the affair."

Richter, in Wagner's presence, preserved the ecstatic expression of a priest before a holy apparition. Standing at a little distance he listened to the Master thoughtfully, his steady eyes shining behind his glasses, in the midst of the abundant gold of his beard and his hair. He seemed to have lost the power of speech. As for Scheffer, seated in a corner, he pulled softly at the ears of the dog crouched between his knees, and watched his glorious guest with a devout air.

Wagner endured, or seemed to endure, these fresh trials with an admirable serenity; he had, as it were, an armour of happiness which the blows of fate would henceforth hit without piercing, and this group of disciples zealous for the faith, seemed to form a rampart about his heart.

Very cheerfully he gave me the news of Tribschen and of the vexations that the Munich events had caused there. The day after the dress rehearsal chanced to be a day of many visitors. " One of his sisters with her husband and daughter; an eminent student of Sanscrit, professor at the University of Leipzig; a philologist of Basle "— that was Nietzsche—so they had a number of people with them at two o'clock dinner. This dinner was interrupted ten times by the arrival of telegrams; the Master left the table in order to write a reply; no sooner had he returned and taken his place, than another message was brought to him and he was forced to absent himself again. All those good people were amazed and could not believe that, ordinarily, in that dear retreat of Tribschen, one saw and heard nothing of the outside world.

By the questions that Wagner asked of Richter concerning certain passages from the score of the *Rheingold*, the effect that they produced, and the sound of new combinations, I comprehended that hardest of all for the composer, in the sacrifice upon which he had determined, was to deny himself from hearing his orchestra : and that without admitting it to himself, perhaps, he believed he should find a balm for this intense desire, in the rehearsal which he had solicited for the following day. Truly, there would be very little opportunity in such a short time, of materially improving the deplorable scenic arrangements. It was evident that the Master had, above all, two things most at heart : to hear his work once, as if by stealth—and to restore Richter, who was without means, to his high position of Capellmeister to the Royal Theatre.

We should see what to-morrow would bring ! Wagner ought to make the attempt, if not to sleep, at least to rest ; Richter and I took leave of him, and left him to the care of the glorified Reinhard Scheffer.

XIX

A brougham drawn by two horses stood before the house in Alte Pferdestrasse, when I went to learn the news the next day.

Feeling that it was sure to be some one from the Court who was in conference with the Master, I did not enter at once, but sauntered away for some little distance, waiting till the interview should be over.

It lasted a long time. Finally I saw Düfflipp, the Court Counsellor, come out, followed by the Director, Perfall. The swarthy and saccharine face of the king's secretary was all shining with perspiration. He wore a suit of chestnut-coloured cloth. His big awkward shoulders disappeared into the carriage, and Perfall, very red and very much given to obsequious bowings, closed the door. The horses reared, stamping noisily on the pavingstones, then pranced off at a great pace, while the Director walked rapidly away.

They both had the aspect of rogues. I hurried up the stairs to Scheffer's floor, urged by anxiety and the desire to know what had happened.

I found Wagner in a peculiar state of mind,

ironically gay, satirical, full of jokes, but calm, without any trace of anger.

" Do you recall that sentence of *King Lear*," he asked me, " ' The worst is not yet,' when they had said : ' this is the worst ' ? To-day surpasses yesterday. Tartufflipp is just gone and the measure is full. Not only do they refuse me the only rehearsal I asked for, and reject Richter (who has failed in the obedience and respect which he owed to such a director as Perfall) forever, but again they drive me away from Munich. I am, it appears, a public menace and my life is in danger. It is terrible ! The poor counsellor was quite distracted about it, his hump shivered with disquietude. . . Truly, if he worries so about me, his health will be affected and, in order to prevent such a misfortune, I must go away at once."

" Oh ! without seeing even one rehearsal of your work ? "

" But the theatre would be quite likely to collapse upon me if I passed its threshold ! Do you not understand ? Tartufflipp comprehends it all very well ; with the greatest solicitude and tenderness he incited me to a prompt flight !

To all that I attempted to say to him, he made the same reply—'But that is not the question, do not remain here, you must not stay, how terrible if anything were to happen to you!'"

" Did he speak in the name of his Master ? "

" Not at all! The King is undoubtedly ignorant of the fact that I am here. I tried to see him, this morning, at his Castle of Berg ; but they told me he had gone on an excursion. There is a guard all about him in order to prevent my approaching him. But I foresee in all this a cause for recriminations which might do harm to the royal person, and in the endeavour to spare him all annoyance I take myself off, without protest. You may be sure that the enormous sum the King has put at the disposal of the theatre has given rise to wrath among the ministers. The fact that this sum has been mis-used, squandered without profit, through the in-capacity and the knavery of those to whom it was confided, does not lessen the complaint against the King. Then let us accept the situation. We will let people imagine if they can that the stage arrangements of the *Rheingold* are superb ; if mincemeat must be made of my work, I

submit to it, if only they will not incriminate
the King, and will leave me alone."

At that moment Richter arrived.

" Master," said he, " I have said my good-byes
to the musicians of the orchestra ; they replied by
a very touching ovation to me, and they begged
me to assure you of their most enthusiastic
loyalty."

" My poor friend," said Wagner, " you are the
real victim of this deplorable fiasco."

But Richter, his eyes sparkling with joy, replied :
" I am happy ! "

Wagner reached out his arms and embraced
him warmly.

" Ah ! Here is Wotan ! " said I—as Betz, the
singer, entered.

" They are pasting up new posters ! " cried
he. " 'The orchestra will be conducted by Herr
Wülner, the rôle of Wotan will be sung by Herr
Betz ! ' Ha ! ha ! do they really believe so ?
Well, the *Rheingold* will neither be given on this
Thursday, nor yet on Sunday, because I have
to tender my farewell to you, Master ; instead
of signing my new engagement with the Royal
Theatre of Bavaria, I am going this evening to

Berlin, without even forewarning that wretch of a Perfall."

XX

The carriage which was to take Wagner to the railway station, on that Thursday the 2nd September, was to come for me before going to the " Old street of horses," and that before daylight, as the train left at 5.15 in the morning.

This time, all the disciples were to be permitted to see the Master—if only they waked early enough—and it was arranged that they should bid him farewell at the station where, in order not to attract attention, each one was to go singly.

The sun was hardly up and it was still chilly in spite of the season, on that high plateau where Munich is situated, when the old hackney coach, driven by a young coachman in blue and with a Tyrolean hat, carried me through the deserted city streets.

At the sound of the little bells and the wheels of the coach, Richter came down with the handbag; then came Wagner followed by Scheffer.

The Master looked very well, and the serenity

of his humour seemed to have increased since
the day before.

After we had started, I complimented him upon
the strength of mind which sustained him in the
face of this disaster, upon his magnanimous
resignation, or perhaps, his Olympian scorn.

"Neither the one nor the other!" said he.
"I have found my force in the belief that nothing
essential, nothing of that which is closest to me,
is hurt by this contention. My work, after the
impression which it has made upon all of you,
who understand me so intimately, must be just
what I wished for it, and it soars away intact
and free, from amidst the tawdry rubbish with
which they try to disguise it.

"There is still another thing; it is that human
malignity is no longer able to reach or hurt me
deeply across the warm affection and the devotion
which surround me. This certainty has comforted
me. You see that even here, as I go away, I
leave friends. You also know with what anxious
tenderness they watch for my arrival at home!
Truly, when I think of the past and the despair
into which such circumstances as these would
have plunged me then, when I had to bear my

pain alone, I am able to feel almost joyous. Stop, look at the excellent Richter ! " added he with a laugh. " he feels as I do, at twenty-eight he loses a position that a mature man would find it difficult to obtain, and, in place of the downcast countenance he ought to have, he shows us a sincere expression of the most complete satisfaction."

As a matter of fact, sitting opposite the Master, Richter, the golden, gazed at him with an air of utter beatitude.

" It is because Richter, he also," say I, " soars above the ' misérabilites,' he even carries a glorious palm, and, like the martyrs of the Coliseum, he sings thanksgivings while the lions are eating him."

" Verily," cried Richter, " I go, like them, straight to Heaven ! "

That was true, for Wagner had " commanded " Richter to go and instal himself at Tribschen and await events there.

As we passed through the Maximilian Square, the Master called attention to a statue with which he was unfamiliar.

" Who is that ? " asked he.

"It is Goethe, by Widnmann," responded Scheffer.

Wagner lifted his soft felt hat and said ;

" It is a striking likeness ! "

Then he added :

" I said that for fun, but I could very well have known Goethe, I must have been about fifteen when he died.   However I should be pleased to make you believe that I am younger than Richter !'

" You are younger, Master ;   the Immortals have no age."

At the station we were all reunited.   There were Villiers, Schuré, Servais and others.   Wagner took them all cordially by the hand and Richter presented to him Franz Servais, whom he did not yet know, but of whom Liszt had often spoken to him.

The train was in readiness, the compartment chosen, some one arranged the luggage.

The Master, in a boyish humour, sat on the floor of the carriage, in the opening of the door, the step serving for his footstool.   We ranged ourselves in a circle, which formed a rampart about him.

I always remember him so under his big gray

felt hat, with his luminous blue eyes, his laughing
mouth, so finely cut above the prominence of the
wilful chin, and the neckerchief of yellow satin
which he had crossed over his throat because of
the chilly morning air.

He reminded us of our promise to go again
and greet him at Tribschen on our way back to
Paris. He also invited Servais to go when we
did.

"Since they have chased me out of Munich,"
said Wagner "those who love me have nothing
further to keep them here."

"We shall remain only a few days," said I,
"to keep an eye on the enemy and to see whether,
furious at his defeat, he may not prepare some
vengeance."

"Bah! the conqueror saves himself and will
be out of reach of his blows. But let it be well
understood that I triumph in spite of myself,
thanks to the generous defection of Betz, that I
did not wish in any case to oppose the will of the
King nor to prevent the representation. As for
you, Richter, do not forget that I only give you
time to go and embrace your mother and to strap
your trunks . . . and then you must come as

fast as possible to Tribschen, where your room
is prepared."

Without responding, Richter seized the Master's
hand and kissed it.

The heartless whistle of the train interrupted
us.   We must separate.   Wagner rose and stepped
into the carriage; the door was closed. Still
leaning from the window, he waved his grey hat;
the wind scattered the locks of his hair about
his splendid forehead, and, as long as the train
remained in sight, we continued to signal with
our handkerchiefs our latest farewell.

XXI

Richter's mother lived in a little village somewhere in the neighbourhood of Munich. He had
planned to pass two or three days with her before
his departure for Lucerne and had asked us to go
with him; he would show us the country and we
should be able to return to Munich the same day
before the evening meal.

Villiers and Servais were of the party. We
passed through pleasant and hilly country,
picturesque with the villages of the suburban
residents.

Frau Richter was a professor of singing, and it was the lesson hour when we entered the little house where she lived. Scales and trills of remarkable shrillness struck our ears, while we waited on the ground floor for the lesson to be over. The pupils passed us on their way out, and Richter conducted us up to the first floor and into the drawing-room, which was well furnished in a homelike and very German fashion.

Frau Richter was still a young woman, of attractive presence and manner. She spoke very regretfully of the events which had led to the dismissal of her son and she seemed to fear that he would never again find so good a position.

They brought us beer and bretzels. The talk languished a little at first, but when Richter told us that his mother had invented a method of singing which increased the power of the voice five-fold, she at once became interested and animated,

In fact, the pupils we had heard just before, had seemed to us to have a very unusual volume of tone.

Frau Richter's method consisted in throwing the sound, when singing, against the vault of the palate, which then forms a sort of drum increasing the resonance and the force of the tone to an astonishing degree.

Richter sat down at the piano and sang according to this method. His voice came out in tremendous volume, making the little house tremble to its foundation.

" One would say that his palate was made of tin," cried Villiers.

Our amiable hostess explained her discovery in detail, illustrating meanwhile in a voice that sounded like a bell.

Servais was the first one to grasp the idea, he tried it and produced some very wonderful bel-lowings.

" The curious thing about it," said Richter, " is that this system which my mother has found, does away with all fatigue. One is able to use the voice indefinitely in this way."

And Richter, to prove the truth of his assertion, sang us the entire third scene from the *Rheingold*.

When we had taken leave of our hosts, and were established in our railway carriage, we made our very best endeavours to sing from the palate, and the result was a scandalous cacophony.

XXII

In governmental circles, the intrigues continued around the incidents occasioned by the *Rhein-gold*, and the journalists who took their cue from there, did not cease to expend their servile ink in writing calumnious articles.

Finally Wagner was constrained to break the silence he had wished to keep, by publishing a short article in the *Allgemeine Zeitung* of Augsburg. He asserted once again in this article that he had never offered any opposition to the execution of his work. " I should certainly be very glad," he wrote, " if they would give up the idea of playing it under such deplorable conditions ; but if they have decided to do so, I am entirely resigned and I have no intention of hindering the representations."

The news from Tribschen informed me that the Master was in good health, but the persistence of this animosity toward him had made even his strength of mind waver for a moment. Cosima had surprised him, one day, alone in his room, seated on a low chair and sobbing. But serenity and cheerfulness soon came back, he applied

o

himself again regularly to the work which he had given up during those days of trouble, and then all went well.

At the theatre, Kindermann—" the singing gun "—as Villiers called him, because of his thundering voice—who interpreted the rôle of one of the giants, studied also that of Wotan, abandoned by Betz.

They had sent to Darmstadt in all haste, for the very skilful decorator, Brandt, and had requested him to patch up the scenery a little if possible, but he fled away more quickly than he came, declaring that he could not do anything with such horrors, that all would have to be remade.

The management did not give up, however, for the *Rheingold* was announced for the 22nd September.

All the visitors who had come to Munich from different countries went away again, one after another. Liszt was the first to go. Without doubt he went secretly to Lucerne to see his daughter. Madame Muchanoff paid us a farewell visit. She herself would pass through Lucerne and make a visit to Wagner. Richter was already at Tribschen and Schuré would also go there.

We were the last to leave Munich, in spite of the anonymous letters which we daily received, threatening us with all sorts of retribution unless we went at once. " It is you who have prevented the theatre from carrying out the King's orders ; you are the servants of a traitor, traitors yourselves. . . . It is not to be endured much longer etc. . . ." But we were not in the least disturbed.

Cosima told me that at one time in Munich she had received each day as many as four or five letters, in which they swore that she should die and called her " Prussian spy."

We remained, chiefly, to give time for the crowd of visitors then at Tribschen to leave, in order that we should not encumber that delicious retreat. Finally they called us back with such a charming and affectionate insistence, assuring us that there was no longer any one there, that we suddenly decided to go.

And, face to the enemy, we quitted Munich, without resentment against that pretty city, where we had received from all those who were not in league with the Court faction, the most sympathetic and cordial welcome.

XXIII

This time, we arrived at Tribschen without being expected.

What joy to know and to return ! to leap from the boat to the landing with its familiar little shed ! to see again with our real eyes, the garden, the house, the lovely verdure, the air so blue. . . .

Servais, who saw it all for the first time, was deeply moved.   Villiers exulted.

I ran across the lawn, to be the first to arrive, Russ discovered us, he bounded forward, recognised me and greeted me with loud barks.

Then the children ran with cries of delight. In the salon, the sound of the piano, which I had heard, suddenly ceased. Wagner appeared at the top of the steps and Cosima followed him.

" Ah ! there you are at last ! " cried he, hurrying down the steps. " Without knowing any thing about it, I expected you to-day ! "

And they embraced us, " Not," as Cosima declared, " like people of the world, but like peasants."

How much they had to tell us, and to re-tell chiefly about the nightmare of the *Rheingold*,

which started up again when they thought it
had subsided and was not yet at an end!

" You can imagine," Cosima said to me, " the
mixture of terror and of joy that overwhelmed
me, when, two days after the Master's departure,
I received the dispatch announcing his sudden
return. I waited for him at the station with
the four children and the two dogs. At the sight
of his radiant expression I was at once reassured,
and the thought that I have something to do
with the serenity he is able to preserve through
all this trouble, makes me feel as happy as it
makes me proud. The moments of weakness
and discouragement which he passed through will
not come any more, and Tribschen will remain
the paradise that you know."

They had had one satisfaction all through these
troubled days : the reconciliation with Liszt,
or rather the end of the misunderstanding.
Cosima confessed, in a low voice, that her father
had come one evening, secretly ; that he had
passed a night at Tribschen, and that this had
been a very sweet consolation. Now they had
cut off all relation with the outer world again,
and they lived for noble labour and domestic joys.

" Do you know how we were occupied when you arrived ? " the Master asked me.

" You were making music, but it did not seem to me to be from Wagner."

" We were playing, Cosima and I, some of Haydn's symphonies, arranged for four hands, and that with the greatest pleasure. We have chosen the twelve English Symphonies, which Haydn wrote after the death of Mozart. For some time we have been following this study and it has given us some delightful hours."

Richter who had been at Tribschen for several days, had undoubtedly heard us arrive. He slipped into the drawing-room almost furtively, and saluted us with a restrained affection.　In Wagner's presence, he always seemed ecstatic and overwhelmed. Cosima assured me that he had been so since his arrival. " One can hardly make him speak. He stays out of sight, for fear of being in the way, renders all sorts of services, goes to bathe the dogs, and, when he is present he stands off in a corner, where he listens and admires. Sometimes he starts away, suddenly, and one can hear him going down to the kitchen. Curious to know what he wanted to do there,

JUDITH GAUTIER IN HER GARDEN AT SAINT EUOGAT.

one evening some one followed without his sus-
pecting it, and heard him relating to the servants
who listened to him open-mouthed, as to a
sermon, all the beautiful things that Wagner
had said ! "

XXIV

To-day they presented to me Siegfried,—
familiarly called " Fidi." He is a splendid
baby, who weighs down the arms of his nurse.
He does not talk yet, but he understands what
is said to him. They ask him :

" Fidi, wie gross bist du ? "

(" Fidi, how big are you ? ")

He holds up his arms and shows, with a laugh
full of dimples, that he is as high as the ceiling.

" Here," said I, " is a little being who has a
very exceptional origin : descendant of Wagner
and Liszt ! What plans of future glory have
they already formed for him ? "

" That is all very vague," said the mother,
laughing. " I have the ambition, first of all,
to assure him a modest income, so he may
always be sheltered from those terrible material
worries, those shameful ' little miseries ' from which
I have suffered so cruelly. Then I should like

to have him know something of surgery, so he
could give help to anyone who was wounded, make
a first dressing. I have so often been grieved
by my own helplessness, when an accident has
happened near me, that I wish to spare him that
pain. Otherwise I shall leave him quite free.
I should be glad, however, if he were to develop
a taste for architecture."

"While we are waiting," added Cosima to me,
"for the future architect to declare himself, do
you feel yourself worthy, dear friend, of fulfilling
a mission of confidence on his behalf ? The nurse
is just going to her dinner, which is served before
ours ; as for me, I have a bath ready which the
sun has warmed ; water heated in that way is
very hygienic ; I should like to take my plunge
right away, in order not to be late for dinner.
Now, this is the hour when Fidi is in the habit
of sucking a biscuit soaked in madeira ; and
there is no one to give it to him but you."

"Madeira at his age ? " I am very much
surprised, but I make no objection, being also
very conscious of my own incompetence.

So here I am installed in the garden, near a
little iron table, on the other side of the curtain

of shrubbery which conceals Cosima's bath. Fidi
is on my knees. Penetrated by the importance
of my task, I soak the biscuit in the madeira,
neither too much nor too little, and I am very
careful not to soil the pretty embroideries of the
robe. The baby eagerly sucks the golden wine
and swallows the biscuit, without coughing or
choking. I am not able to see, but behind the
leaves I hear the splashing of the water and Cosima's
voice encouraging me. All goes well, as long
as the madeira and the biscuit last. But when
there is nothing more, Fidi gives manifest signs
of impatience. He twists himself about, in order
to escape and slide to the ground. Shall I let
him go? Never! I am not authorised. I
do not even know if he can walk by himself.
But he is quite determined to get down, kicks
vigorously, and looks at me with frowning brows,
as though he were astonished that I do not
understand.

" Do hurry, Cosima, Fidi detests me and wishes
to get away."

" No indeed, he loves you very much," cried
the bather, " hold him tight."

So I hold him tight, but he has incredible

strength and a persevering will. The struggle is painful and long . . . finally, when they come to my aid, it becomes evident, too late, that the baby had serious reasons for his determination to get down.

XXV

This morning, Richard Wagner received a letter from the celebrated Pasdeloup. . . .

It will be remembered, perhaps, that at this time, Pasdeloup had been director of the Theatre Lyrique for rather more than a year. He had, as a matter of course, produced at his theatre, first of all, one of Wagner's operas, and as he intended to play them all in succession he had begun with *Rienzi*, the first as to date. The work had been brilliantly mounted and well received, and the tenor, Monjauze, really remarkable in the rôle of the Tribune, had had a very decided success.

In his letter of to-day, Pasdeloup wrote that *Rienzi* was to be given again at the re-opening of the theatre, but without Monjauze, who had unfortunately broken his arm.

They begrudged Monjauze and regretted exceedingly that it was necessary to replace him, for he alone, in that work, was equal to his part. Pasdeloup did not say who would take his place.

It was on the occasion of that first representation of *Rienzi* at Paris, that, urged by Pasdeloup, I had written again to Wagner,—after the sending of the famous articles which had brought me the beautiful response from the Master, in which he explained to me certain scenes from the *Meistersinger* — I wrote this time, to ask if he would not like to come to Paris to stage and direct this work. He replied to me with a second letter, equally beautiful and very dignified, intended for publication and which appeared in *La Liberté*.

" Now that I know your writing," said I to Cosima, " I realise that the letter was by your own hand."

" That is true, Wagner wrote it first in German. I translated it into French, then we re-read it and corrected it together, and finally I copied it again."

" How wrong of us to have given you all that trouble ! Pasdeloup was over-confident. If I had known about this retreat of Tribschen, how

sacrilegious would have seemed to me the idea
of asking the Master to leave it in order to please
a Theatre Director ! "

" You have seen by the affair of the *Rheingold,*
that it is much better for Wagner not to mingle
with the theatrical world. His first duty is
to keep his creative faculty intact, but he is a
' fighter,' and is always tempted to throw himself
into the fray."

" Now that I have the joy of knowing him,
he will never again be called to battle by me ! "

" He will return of himself, only too soon, for
repose is not for him," added Cosima, sighing.

" I am curious to read again that letter that
you wrote, you two, when you believed me to
be a very serious old lady. . . . Do you remember
your surprise, the first time you saw me to find me
so different from what you had imagined ?   You
would not be able to write in the same tone now."

" Certainly, the style of your articles does
not at all resemble you, and we did not in the
least foresee the *gamin* that you are . . . sometimes ! "

" Neither could I have known that Wagner
climbed trees. . . ."

" But in any case the letter had nothing private in it; it was written to be published."

Cosima had kept a copy of the text, which she found, and we read it together :—

" Madame,

" You are kind enough to ask me for some details relating to the time of my first stay in France, with the kindly intention of writing an article by their aid, the publication of which shall coincide with my arrival in Paris, which you believe to be near. While thanking you for the interest which you are so kind as to feel for me, permit me to say, Madame, that it is not my intention to go to Paris. I know that I have excellent friends, indeed, even numerous friends there, and I hope I do not need to assure you that I am capable of appreciating the value and the importance of the testimonies of sympathy of which I am the object. Nevertheless my presence and my participation in the representation that is being prepared might very well give rise to a misunderstanding. It would appear as though I were putting myself at the head of a theatrical enterprise with the intention of regaining by *Rienzi* that which I have lost by *Tannhäuser*. At least it would undoubtedly be in this way that the Press would interpret my going. Whereas the stage setting of *Rienzi* at the Théâtre Lyrique has only been an entirely personal question between M. Pasdeloup and me.

"After the production of the *Meistersinger* at Munich, and the attention it attracted, many propositions were made to me. At first they spoke of sending a German troupe, to give my six operas, one after another, in Paris; then some one wished to attempt *Lohengrin* in Italian, then again *Lohengrin* in French, and so on. In short, there were no less than five projects that summer, concerning the representations of my works in Paris. Yet I did not encourage any one of them. When M. Pasdeloup told me that he had accepted the directorship of the Théâtre Lyrique with the intention of giving several of my works, I did not feel that I could refuse to this zealous and capable friend, the authorisation for bringing them out; and, as he desired to begin with *Rienzi*, I said to him that, in fact, of all my operas, that one had always seemed to me best adapted to the French stage. Written, thirty years ago, with a view to Grand Opera, *Rienzi* does not present so many difficulties to the singers, nor will it offer to the Parisian public so much that is unusual as the works which have followed it. Both in subject and in musical form, it is closely related to the operas that have been popular in Paris for a long time, and I still believe that, if it is richly mounted and given with spirit, it has a chance of success. That success I wish for it with all my heart, and still more success to my friend M. Pasdeloup, who, of his own free will, has valiantly and energetically upheld my cause for a number of years. But I should be unwise to wish to contribute to that success by my presence. My nature as well as my destiny have decreed for me the concentration and the solitude of work, and I feel myself to be absolutely unfit for any exterior enterprise. Either *Rienzi* will make its way without me, or, if it is not capable of doing so, my assistance cannot help it and we can only suppose that the conditions are unfavourable.

"Such is, in a few words, my point of view

and the line of conduct which I have decided, or rather, which I am called upon to follow, with regard to the representation of my works in Paris, whichever they may be. And please, Madame, do not see in this reserve any sign of unreasonable disdain, which could be assumed to mask a deeper feeling of rancour. I am very far from pooh-poohing a Paris success, and I even assure you that I have always considered it one of the numerous ironies of my fate that *Rienzi*, composed within sight of Paris, was not given there long ago, when that work of my youth still held for me all its freshness. But, since you speak of the renown that I have acquired in Germany, permit me to tell you, Madame, that all such renown has come without my personal participation, with the help only of a few friends, in the midst of the howls of the entire Press of the North and of the South. It has come because of my works alone, and in spite of the obstacles that my political situation opposed to the extended knowledge of my operas. It is in the same way that I wish to succeed in Paris, where I have found very devoted friends, who are too intelligent for me to fear to leave the fate of my works in their hands. If you were to say to me, Madame, that a representation ought to conform to my intentions, and therefore my presence at the rehearsals would be above all necessary to the success of the enterprise, I should reply to you that *Tannhäuser* and *Lohengrin* have been mutilated by the greater number of German Capellmeisters, in a way that could not be exceeded upon the worst French stage, and that is only since the King of Bavaria has accorded me his protection that it has been possible for me to make my dramatic and musical intentions known in an important theatre.

" Believe me, Madame, things being as they are, there is nothing for me to do but devote myself entirely to the writing of my operas, and as to their fate, in my own country as well as abroad, to leave it to their guiding star and to my friends. I am not the man for compromises, and yet these compromises are sometimes indispensable.

" I keep out, then, in order not to render more difficult to my French friends the rugged path they have chosen in attempting to naturalise in France an essentially Germanic individuality. If this naturalisation is possible, it will be accom-

P

plished by them without my help; if it is
not possible, I shall deplore their pains, at
the same time consoling myself in the thought
that they as well as I have drawn their forces
elsewhere than from the idea of a success, and
that their conviction, like mine, renders them
independent of good or of bad fortune.

"Pray, Madame, pardon the length of this,
explanation, and believe me gratefully and
respectfully yours,

"RICHARD WAGNER."

"The Master was nevertheless, very well satisfied with the success of the piece," said Cosima,
"and above all, with the expressions of apprecia-
tion that it won for him from unknown friends.
Then too, in order to celebrate his birthday,
the 22nd May—inspired by one of the most
popular scenes in the opera—I dressed the children
as 'Messengers of Peace' and while an invisible
choir sang for them, the little girls, all four of
them, marched, keeping step with one another,
into the drawing-room with travelling staffs in
their hands. Wagner thought it a very pretty
idea."

" Eva as a messenger of peace must have been
delicious. . . ."

" I also preserved your father's article about
Rienzi,[1] which was very good," said Cosima.
" Wagner ought to have written to thank him."

" If they represent *Rienzi* again," said I, " we
shall also faithfully renew our pilgrimage to the
theatre. Think of us then, two and a half weeks
from now, as going every day from the heart of
Neuilly to the Théâtre Lyrique, and never failing
to be in our places in time for the Overture ! "

ARTICLE PUBLISHED IN THE " JOURNAL
OFFICIEL "

Rarely has Parisian curiosity been more vividly
excited than by the following simple words
inscribed upon the placards of the " Théâtre-
Lyrique."

Tuesday, first representation of Rienzi,
Opera in five Acts, by Richard Wagner.

In an age when the general interest is certainly
not with works of art, Wagner has the gift of
stimulating the public, of calling forth frantic
enthusiasms and provoking violent repulsions.

The mere mention of his name assembles clouds
in the most serene heavens, clouds which soon
grow into a storm, lightning breaks out in
intermittent flashes, thunder mutters and growls
above the sound of the rain, the wind and the
hail.   In all this tumult no one remains indifferent,
the universe seems about to collapse and each
person hurries toward the altar of his own menaced
deity.

The rival choruses of detractors and admirers
insult each other as at the taking of Messina and
are ready to tear each other to pieces.   There
is an excitement,—a tumult—a fury, which recalls the great romantic struggles of 1830, when
the young followers of Hernani broke into the
theatre with their password, and tore away
the classic masks and headgear—proclaiming the
liberty and independence of art.

If we had never heard a note of Richard Wagner,
all this uproar would have assured us of his
superiority.   He troubled all the musical world
too profoundly not to be a genius, a hero, in
accordance with the meaning of Emerson and
Carlyle.   From whatever point of view one con-
siders him, he always produces a new sensation,

it may be a little prematurely, but one is conscious even now that he will become the sovereign master and that nothing can prevent his future greatness. Very soon his victorious banner will float from the highest turret of the citadel, gilded by the sun and caressed by the very wind which before had twisted and torn it.

Young musicians, not yet established, regard Wagner either as a God or as a tempting demon. It is Wagner who preoccupies the thoughts of the older masters already secure in their own glory, and in every contemporaneous work it is not difficult to find some reflections, or at least traces of the secret study of this powerful originator.

A chance of travel led to my being present at a production of Tannhäuser in the theatre at Wiesbaden, at a time, already long past, when the name of Richard Wagner was hardly mentioned in France. This music, strikingly novel to us who knew absolutely nothing of the composer, made an impression upon us at the same time strange and delicious. We had heard for the first time the true music of romance, such as poets might conceive it. The opera reproduced,

with most unaffected fidelity, the legend of the
good knight Tännhauser and Madame Venus,
living happily together on the heights of Venusberg
—until at last the noble German, who was a good
Catholic at heart, became suspicious of some
witchcraft and said to his mythological companion :

" Venus, my beautiful Goddess,
Thou art in truth a demon."

That which most impressed us in the score
of the Teutonic Master was the extreme clearness
of the musical manner of translating the spoken
phrase by means of a continuous melody, without elaboration, without superfluous flourish, the
orchestra providing the commentary, and sustain-
ing with its own fulness the simplicity of the
vocal design. We sent from Wiesbaden either
to the " Moniteur " or the " Artiste," we no
longer remember which, an appreciative article
which ended in expressing astonishment that an
opera so original and unusual had not yet passed
beyond the limits of the Rhine. Our astonishment
was also great when, some years later, this same
Tannhäuser—so easily given at the theatre of
Wiesbaden, by singers and an orchestra which

were probably not the first in Germany—having
been produced here at the Opera, was declared
impossible, foolish, absurd, outside all the possibilities of the theatre, and was smothered
under a storm of hisses. They muffled Wagner's
music in derisive purple, under the pleasantry
" Music of the Future," but the wag who invented
the phrase had no idea that he spoke so truly.
In fact its time has come, and the music of the
future is very near to being the music of to-
day. The fall of Tannhäuser in no way unsettled
our convictions. Critics are stubborn, and even
though they are not dealing with the old romantic
poets, they know very well that hisses do not
kill a work of genius.

They said of the dramatic verses of Victor
Hugo precisely what they say of the musical
phrases of Wagner. Accusing them conclusively
of not being verse at all, yet to-day it is a common
argument of advance that the author of " Ruy-
Blas " and the " Légende des Siècles " is the
greatest master of metrical form of our time.

But to return to Rienzi, the production of which
at the Théâtre-Lyrique accomplished an old-
time project of the Master's. One of Wagner's

letters makes that clear—" Written about thirty years ago, with a view to grand opera, Rienzi presents no difficulties for the singers to overcome, and offers to the Parisian public none of the problems of my later works. Both in subject and in musical form it is closely related to the operas that have long been popular in Paris, and I still believe that if it is brilliantly mounted and given with spirit it has a chance of success."

For serious works, time is required in which to bring them a full acknowledgment, but it comes at last, and the Master's own judgment of his work was most triumphantly confirmed the other evening. Rienzi has not literally arrived at the Grand Opera, but at the Théâtre-Lyrique it met with a zeal, an ardonr of conviction and a passionate devotion which ought to banish from his mind any possible regret. Pasdeloup has splendidly welcomed the illustrious guest that he endeavours to introduce and to naturalize in France.

A few words upon the libretto translated from Wagner's poem by Messrs Mütter and Guillaume. One need not seek there for the learned complications of our own lyric dramas. It is the history of Rienzi very simply told just as it happened in reality. Cola Gabrino, called "Rienzi" or "Rienzo," was the son of an Innkeeper. He received a good education, bound himself in friendship with Petrarch and, in studying antiquity, became enamoured of the ideas of liberty and a republic. The sojourn of the Popes at Avignon delivered Rome over to the most troublesome disorders. Rienzi harangued the people, succeeded in making himself Tribune, drove out the Barons and re-established the old and good government. His rule at first was wise, but intoxicated by too great power after having been liberator he became the oppressor of Rome. Driven out of the city once, he returned and was killed in a riot, by a servitor of the house of Colonna. Beginning like Brutus, he ended like Masaniello or Jean de Leyde.

Rienzi, Wagner's first lyric drama, shows already an immense talent. Here is not yet revealed the Wagner of the Flying Dutchman, but a man, nevertheless, untrammelled by precedent. Excepting the Cavatinas in the Italian style, inserted here and there to please the public, the opera resembles no other, the impression

is unique. It is all a great tumult, a rising of
the people. There are in fact only two characters, Rienzi and the populace. It is more like
a magnificent symphony with choruses than like
an opera as ordinarily heard. The orchestra
has become the great power, the science of which
the composer fully understands and controls.

In the first act, the call to arms—

" When the trumpet shall have sounded thrice,"

is marked by a proud enthusiasm which extends
to the chorus, whose voices carry on the theme
swelling and augmenting it to a superb crescendo.
The trio which follows is intermingled with an
adorable accompaniment. In the second act
the aria sung by the first of the messengers
of peace, felicitating Rienzi, was warmly and
insistently applauded. Nothing could be more
sweet, more tender or more delicate than this
melody, admirably sung by Mlle. Priolat, from
whom the entire audience demanded its repetition.

The chorus of conspiring patricians is also
very fine; under the dull murmurs one divines
the revolt of injured pride and the muttering
of an, as yet, powerless hatred. The entrance

and the grief of Adriano, are expressed in the orchestra by two notes of the hautboys which are like the sigh of a broken heart. This pure and charming detail foretells the later Wagner whose orchestra is able to reveal all things and to make one experience all emotion. The septet and the final chorus are fragments of such power and grandeur that you feel as though you were floating upon wings. In the third act, we especially noted the military march with its firm and warlike rhythm ; and the prayer of the women, augmented in its fervour and its terror by the intermittent sounds of battle. In the fourth act, the march of peace and the magnificently dramatic situation of Rienzi, accursed, excommunicated, deserted, alone upon the steps of the church. In the fifth act, the prayer of Rienzi, admirable in its sadness and its fervour.

> " Rise, O Sun, and make the light of liberty to shine upon the world."

In this part one again sees the powerful Wagner of to-day, and the entrance of the Sister of the Tribune, who consoles him by her devoted love, is like a vista through which one catches a brief

glimpse of the angels with fluttering wings of the
prelude to Lohengrin. One must congratulate
M. Pasdeloup, the new director of the Théâtre-
Lyrique, who has already done so much for art
by means of his popular concerts, for having pro-
produced Rienzi. The notable success of the
first representation, a success which will, undoubtedly, continue, allows us to hope that we may
also have before very long, The Flying Dutchman,
Tannhäuser, Lohengrin, Tristan and Isolde, Die
Meistersinger, and all that unknown repertory,
rich casket of new treasure.

Rienzi is sumptuously mounted, the costumes
and decorations are rich and appropriate; the
choruses well arranged and the whole forms a
splendid spectacle. The final tableau of the death
of Rienzi on his balcony is presented in a highly
dramatic manner.

Montjauze, in his impersonation of Rienzi,
surpasses all one's expectations, he is transfigured
into a singer and an actor of the first rank. This
role is for him what William Tell was for Duprez.
He sustains with wonderful ease the continuous
dialogue with the chorus. His voice dominates
those great, those formidable crowds, and with

a gesture he restrains the flood of people pressing about him in a transport of eagerness and joy. He wears with artistic grace and majesty the splendid white draperies, richly embroidered in gold, with which the Tribune clothed himself in his vanity as a parvenu whose head was turned at the summit of his grandeur. One could not imagine a more perfect incarnation of the type of Rienzi.

Mme. Borghese sings with warmth the rather thin arias of Adriano, lover of the Tribune's sister, who is herself very gracefully represented by Mdlle. Steinberg. But this poor little love episode is tossed about, in all senses, like a drowned flower by the tumultuous foaming upheaval of this great tragic drama, which begins with a battle and ends with a riot.

The choruses are excellent, and the orchestra executes with splendid spirit that overture of Rienzi, already popular long before the opera itself was known.

THÉOPHILE GAUTIER.

XXVI

As Cosima and I, seated on a garden bench, were peacefully talking, Jacob came to us bearing a telegram.

One always trembles before opening a message of this kind.

" It is nothing ! Only rather a bore ! " said Cosima, after reading it. " Two elderly people, named Schott, husband and wife, announce that they will visit us this evening after supper. They are very worthy people, but he, at one time, did Wagner a serious wrong, and Wagner, without exactly holding resentment, yet has not been able to forget. Moreover, these good people are very narrow and stiff, not at all talkative : we shall not know what to do, it will be dull, and all our pleasant, sympathetic atmosphere will be disturbed."

" It might be possible," said I, " to think of something collective that would lessen the necessity for talking during this evening."

" True enough, but what ? "

" You might have some music."

" Wagner would not feel like it, I know him :

under such circumstances he does not know at
all how to dominate, but he grows listless and
loses his good humour."

" That mustn't be ! " I exclaimed. " It is
absolutely necessary to think of something ! "

" Ah yes ! Do help us out of it if possible,
but do not count upon me, I feel utterly incapable of an idea that would be in the least
amusing."

I saw Servais in the distance with Richter,
they were by the edge of the lake, under the little
landing shed, and were throwing bits of wood
into the water, to induce Russ and Cos to take
their bath.

" I believe a light is dawning in my mind,"
said I to Cosima. " Wait for me where you are."

And I ran down to join the two young men at
the edge of the lake.

" My friends," I said to them, " in the face
of a delicate situation do you feel the moral force
to do something unusual, grand, heroic ? "

" Not at all, not at all." replied Servais. " I
don't feel equal to anything of the kind."

" Not in the service of the Master ? "

" One can always try," said Richter.

" That is something like !   Now you see, Servais, you can't get out of it. We must improvise a first class charade for this evening."

" A charade !   Before Wagner, we two alone ? "

" With Richter at the piano."

" But we shall be absurd !   We shall be speechless, like idiots."

" On the other hand the presence of the Master will inspire us.   Moreover, we have had experience at your house in Munich, and it is very certain that only we two (you especially) have shown any talent of this kind."

" It is foolish, impossible, abominable," groaned Servais, in the depths of dismay. " I would rather throw myself into the lake."

" It is not a drama that they want of us, but a farce. . . . Oh, come, they will not be critical, and perhaps we shall have the glory of amusing the Master."

He raised his head abruptly, tucking his pale yellow locks behind his ears :

" Very well, so be it.   Let us play a charade ! "

" Ah, good !   We must have everything arranged before supper.   Let me tell the good news to Madam Cosima, and then we must get to work ! "

" I see that you have thought of something," said Cosima, when I returned to her.

" Yes, we will play a charade."

" A charade ? Splendid ! I do not know exactly what that is, but I am sure that it is something good."

" As to that, you must risk the pillage of your wardrobe."

" I risk it. They shall open the cupboards and the drawers for you. Take anything you like, except, perhaps, my India shawl, which I cherish very much. . . . But you must tell me exactly what you are going to do, so I can explain it all to Wagner ; otherwise he would torture his mind in the effort to comprehend. . . . I am sure that he hasn't the slightest idea what a charade may be ! "

The drawing-room was deserted, so it was possible for Richter, Servais and me to gather round the piano, and with the greatest secrecy to think out, to discuss and to arrange our foolishness.

The music would be a great help to us in representing characters, crowds, uproars and riots. Therefore Richter's rôle was very important,

Q

and as, once the charade had commenced, he
would be separated from us, we agreed upon
certain signals that we should all recognise.

The gallery, with its large opening into the
drawing-room, was chosen for our stage : its
heavy portières, drawn back or dropped, formed
the curtain. All was arranged, the lamps disposed in the right places, the accessories gathered
together. Our greatest difficulty was to induce
the servants to let us have a kettle and a
broom from the kitchen, two objects that
were indispensable to our stage setting. The
cook, throwing up her arms, cried that it was not
at all suitable to take such things to the drawing-
room, so we were obliged to take them by main
force.

XXVII

We had hardly finished supper and were
still at table when Herr and Frau Schott were
announced.

Wagner made a droll face, got up, and offered
me his arm to pass to the drawing-room.

But just outside the door I slipped away, and
with Servais I climbed to the first floor, where

Cosima's maid was waiting to help us do the best we could with our costumes.

When we were ready Jacob lighted the stage lamps; and drawing the curtains a little, we peeped into the drawing-room.

There they are, seated in rows, the two new guests in the front row. They appear to us very solemn and terrifying: two portraits by Franz Hals—a Franz Hals who would have lived under Louis Philippe—tall, straight, all clothed in black; he, in a frock coat and high satin cravat; she, in a dull, lifeless frock, with hardly a line of white at the neck; thin figures and sallow skins; nothing playful about them. We are a little disconcerted. Pshaw! The Master's voice sounds laughingly: he is in a good humour, all goes well. Courage!

Dum! Dum! Dum!

Richter at the piano begins a fanciful overture where the motifs of *Tristan and Isolde* mingle with foreign airs. The curtain is drawn.

A young Chinese lady embroiders under the lamp; but this virtuous occupation and tranquil appearance are deceitful: violent passions agitate her soul. She is married to a man whom she detests, first, just because she detests him, and then because he belongs to a conquering race. He is a Tartar. She waits for her lover, whom she adores, and who himself is a true Chinaman.

The husband is asleep, the night dark; the lover watches in the shadow. Now the hour has come for the signal: she opens the window and waves her scarf. From the piano comes the second act of *Tristan*.

The lover enters impetuously.

" My beloved ? "

" My darling, art thou truly mine ? "

" Dost thou still belong to me ? "

" Are these thine eyes ? "

" Is this thy mouth ? "

" Thy heart ? "

" Sweetheart ! "

" Stem of the Lotus ! "

" Duck of a Mandarin ! "

The music changes. It is now from the fifth scene of *Die Walküre*; enter Sieglinde and Siegmund.

" Is he asleep ? "

" Ah, he sleeps profoundly. I prepared for him an intoxicating drink."

" His sleep is not yet profound enough. Let us finish what thou hast begun : that he may never waken again."

They decide then to assassinate the Tartar, and to conceal his body.

The lover steals into the next room, from which cries are very soon heard, and the sound of a struggle; then the murderer returns, dragging after him an inanimate body.

They must dispose of it, throw it into the river, and the lover tries to pull the dead man onto his back. But this Tartar, who was a man of importance with the rank of Mandarin, had been altogether too well fed and he is horribly heavy, so that the Chinaman is doubled up under his great bulk, and try as he may he cannot carry the unwieldy corpse.

" Ah well, cut him in two ! "

Then, by the aid of a great sabre and their own tremendous efforts, they hack the Tartar in two—not very difficult really, considering the cushions of which he is formed. When this has been accomplished the lover wraps one of the halves in a rug and carries it off. He will come back for the remainder the next night. . . .

Villiers, in the drawing-room, has already guessed that this first syllable which we have acted ought to be " Tar "—the half of a Tartar !

The next thing to do is to make them recognise the illustrious Pasdeloup directing a " popular concert " and that difficult task falls to my lot. I have made myself a beard with skeins of yellow silk, and donned an evening coat of Wagner's. Servais has to multiply himself to represent the public, the police, etc., while Richter in the distance is the orchestra.

All join in giving the " la "[1] with especial significance : then they begin the prelude to *Lohengrin*. Pasdeloup, according to his custom, rounds his back, wrinkles his good-natured face, extends his arms with gestures half supplicating, half soothing, in order to secure " Pianissimi " full of mystery, and the orchestra does his best to obey. But all is not in harmony in the audience. Murmurs arise, are hushed down, then an altercation follows, with a sound of slaps, and swells to an uproar—as it had so often done during those days at " The Cirque d'Hiver."[2]—

[1] " La " A, given for the tuning of the instruments.
[2] A well-known place of entertainment in Paris.

The orchestra stops, the guard drags out the roysterers, and Pasdeloup makes a speech to the public.

And that, both good and bad, represents the syllable " La."

All the servants at Tribschen are crowded at the doors, and they watch this unprecedented sight with devout amazement. At the third scene their attention redoubles, for the kettle and the broom are about to play their part, to the great horror of the cook.

" If it had only been a nice hair broom ! But that ugly old one used to sweep the court ! "

In reality the broom is not exactly the right thing, but as there is only one of me to personate the three witches of Macbeth, I feel that this classic mount will aid the illusion. With my hair concealed under a grey veil, I bestride the diabolical steed, which then proceeds to prance.

> " Round about the cauldron go ;
> In the poison'd entrails throw
> Toad, that under cold stone,
> Days and nights hast thirty-one
> Swelter'd venom sleeping got,
> Boil thou first i' the charméd pot.
> Double, double, toil and trouble ;
> Fire, burn : and, cauldron, bubble.

Fillet of a fenny snake,
In the cauldron boil and bake ;
Eye of newt, and toe of frog,
Wool of bat, and tongue of dog,
Adder's fork, and blind-worm's sting,
Lizard's leg, and owlet's wing,
For a charm of powerful trouble,
Like a hell-broth boil and bubble."

Then comes Macbeth : he is welcomed by the prophetic words :

" All hail, Macbeth, hail to thee thane of Glamis ! "

" Hail to thee, thane of Cawdor ! "

" All hail, Macbeth, that shalt be king hereafter."

And the audience is supposed to understand that the third syllable is " Tane."

We are very successful up to this point. Wagner, who is standing behind an easy chair, leaning his elbows on the back, looks and listens with extreme attention, he is greatly interested and laughs heartily

Now we must give the entire word : " Tarlatane." The public approbation encourages us, so we are no longer nervous about our effects.

Richter plays a waltz.

A lady comes home at midnight from a ball, in a tarlatan frock. Standing before her mirror she begins to remove her jewels, to take the flowers from her hair, meanwhile thinking over the incidents of the evening, the compliments, the scandals, the toilettes more or less pretty, the little absurdities of her friends, which are still amusing her.

As she has danced all the evening, she is very tired, and rejoices at the idea of retiring.

But suddenly there is a ring at the bell. The lady starts :

" Who can be ringing at my house at such an hour ? "

The domestics are in bed. At first she dares not open the door : but she must, for perhaps some one of her neighbours is ill and in need of her.

On the threshold appears a strange young man, tall, thin, with weeping willow locks, and an awkward and conceited air.

" You are no doubt mistaken in the floor, sir, as I have not the honour of your acquaintance."

" How, Madam, you do not remember me ! You know me very well, nevertheless. We have met in society, and I came here once to a Soirée at your house. Let me give you my card ! "

" Ah, yes, I do seem to remember, you are

not altogether a stranger. . . . But what serious
thing can have happened to bring you to my
house so late ? ''

" Oh, do not be disturbed, there is nothing
serious, nothing at all. I was passing your house
by chance; happening to look up, I saw a light
in your window. I said to myself: 'Stay! I
owe this lady a visit, a very much delayed visit,
which must not be put off any longer. . . . What
a good opportunity! Certainly, I am not
sleepy, and, since she is awake she is not sleepy
either. She will be pleased to see me and to
pass a few hours in intellectual conversation
with me.'"

" A few hours ! "

" But, I beg you, do not inconvenience
yourself for me ! do not remain standing; let
us be seated ; one can talk so much better sitting
down."

" But don't you understand, sir, it is very late ! "

" Oh ! do not be disturbed about that, I am
not in the slightest hurry."

And the intruder enters upon a trifling and
endless gabble in spite of the impatience of the
lady, who does not attempt to conceal her ill-

humour, and replies ironically and as briefly as possible. Finally she declares :

" I truly believe that you have lost your common-sense."

" What, do you imagine that I am intoxicated ? Ah well, you will see that is quite impossible when I tell you that I have dined at home : a plain and frugal dinner, of which I retain a very unpleasant memory, and while we are on that subject, I beg of you to be good enough to give me a tooth-pick."

" A tooth-pick ! "

" Yes, exactly, you will in that way do me a favour, because, at that dinner, I partook of veal, and I should very much like a tooth-pick. You see it was paternal veal, stringy, tough and salted. . . . Ah, so salt that I am dying of thirst, and it would be so kind of you if you would have some drinks served."

During the last intermission, some champagne had been uncorked. Wagner, who was as amused as a child, interrupted the scene at this point, crying out :

" Here it is !   Here it is ! "

And he poured the sparkling wine for us himself !

Then Servais became epic.

" It is very curious, Madam, but you have a butler who has a marvellous resemblance to a composer of whom they have been talking very much of late, a certain Richard Wagner. He is an extravagant person, a madman, who makes terrible music, full of discords that are worthy of cannibals and calls it ' the music of the future.' "

And he retailed, without trembling, all the venomous imbecilities that were current, and finally : . . .

" And it appears that this music has no airs, yet, apropos of this, something surprises me very much : this composer has brought out in Paris a so - called opera, which naturally was finely hissed, and which furnished a subject for endless witticisms : one, among others, you might, perhaps, be able to explain to me. Some one said, ' He bores me with his recitatives and wearies me with his airs '—(il me *tanne aux airs*).[1] But since there are no airs ? and then ' tanne.' What can that word mean ? "

[1] Allusion of that time to " Tannhäuser."
" Il m' ennuie aux recitatifs et il me tanne aux airs."

Then the lady's wrath broke forth :

" Sir, ' *tanner*' is a slang word, which means ' to annoy, to bore, to exasperate ' in polite speech. It is, for example, what you are doing here at this moment. I have given proof of extraordinary patience because I am a gentlewoman, but now that you dare to speak offensively of a man whom I believe to be the greatest genius that ever existed, that I will not endure. You have wounded my dearest convictions. You are an idiot and a ruffian, and I have the pleasure of showing you the door, and of charging you never to come to my house again."

Wagner laughed till he cried.

It was necessary to explain, in the midst of the bravos and the recalls, that the word of the charade was " Tarlatane " : A lady in a tarlatane dress . . . a man who " tard la tanne," " stays late and bores."

XXVIII

After having resumed our usual clothing, we went down again to the drawing-room. The Master came to meet us, and pretending not to have recognised us through our disguises, he cried :

" Heavens! where have you been? Why are you so late? We had here a troupe of wonderful comedians, who played the drollest possible piece. . . . How unfortunate that you missed them! You will never see anything like it again!"

As to the worthy visitors, the prime cause of this unique representation, sober, imperturbable, upright in their chairs, in their severe costumes, they sat without moving, listening intently, watching with all their eyes, but probably understanding very little.

I feel sure that they remained forever convinced that it was all from some new work of the Master— some unpublished fragment, perhaps from the *Ring of the Nibelung*!

.   .   .   .   .

And now again it was the farewell evening.

In order to soften the bitterness, Wagner took a score and went to the piano.

" To-day," said he, " let us make peace with the *Meistersinger*."

The Master believed, in spite of my efforts to convince him to the contrary, that I did not care for the *Meistersinger*. The truth is,

that all I had heard of the opera was a few
fragments played at the popular concerts or
at the piano. All that I knew delighted me,
but Wagner would not believe it.

"I do not want you to misunderstand this
work," said he, as he opened the book.

And, for several hours he went through the
score, playing, explaining, commenting with
wonderful kindness.

The music of the *Meistersinger* is especially
difficult to render at the piano and Wagner was
not a very skilful performer—Richter knew that,
so he was very restless and followed the Master's
playing, note by note, with the greatest anxiety.
He knew it all, even the most uninteresting
passages ; he touched the notes that the hand
of the Master was too small to include. From
time to time he was carried out of himself, and
struck the piano hurriedly, saving an effect which
was in danger of being lost, completing a harmony,
or striking a chord between the Master's hesitating
fingers.

I am not sure that Wagner was not a little
irritated by this infringement upon his territory.
It was quite useless, moreover, for no virtuoso

could have been able to render the deep meaning
and secret tenderness of the work as well as its
author. How grateful we were! How completely
the *Meistersinger* was absolved. On that point
Wagner had no longer any doubts.

XXIX

Then they sketched out some new projects.
Servais was in friendly relations with the director
of the "Theâtre de la Monnaie" at Brussels,
and also with Brassin, director of the Conservatory,
who was a Wagnerian fanatic : they wished,
with the Master's permission, to try to arrange
for the production of *Lohengrin* at Brussels, with
Richter as chief of the orchestra.

"If Richter is able to make any money out
of the affair, and in that way to repay himself
for what he has lost through me, I agree to it,"
said Wagner, "but only on that condition."

They gave us some commissions for Paris.
Cosima wanted some preserves "such as one
finds in the Paris grocers' shops." She also
wished me to take a subscription to the journal
called *La Poupée Modèle*, for Senta.

Wagner had been for a long time searching for a particularly delicious snuff, which could, no doubt, be found at " La Civette."

" For," said he, " while it is true that I smoke, I also take snuff sometimes, from a beautiful golden snuff box, like an ancient Marquis. . . . So you see, I have all the vices, but in moderation."

We tried not to be sad. We had gathered a bountiful harvest of memories, and we were consoled by our just pride in such a wonderful friendship.

Moreover they promised us frequent news. Cosima, " who writes letters like Madame de Sévigné," would be punctual and faithful, " provided always that one replied to her as faithfully."

We would continue then to hold firmly on high the banner of Art, to fight the good fight, up to the final triumph of our cause.

And, after the farewell kiss, we went away, stoical, bearing with us much happiness :

Aux pèlerins d'amour
La vision du dieu parfume le retour !

R

EXTRACT FROM ONE OF WAGNER'S LETTERS TO MADAME GAUTIER, SHOWING PART OF SCORE OF THE FIRST ACT IN "PARSIFAL."

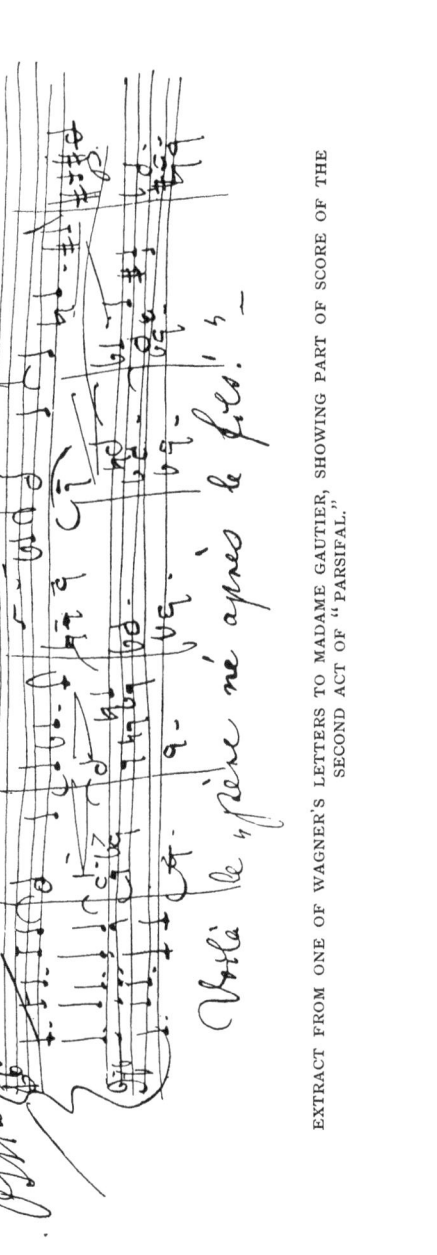

EXTRACT FROM ONE OF WAGNER'S LETTERS TO MADAME GAUTIER, SHOWING PART OF SCORE OF THE
SECOND ACT OF "PARSIFAL."

For EU product safety concerns, contact us at Calle de José Abascal, 56–1°,
28003 Madrid, Spain or eugpsr@cambridge.org.

www.ingramcontent.com/pod-product-compliance
Ingram Content Group UK Ltd.
Pitfield, Milton Keynes, MK11 3LW, UK
UKHW040617240426
470322UK00010B/165